# WILD ABOUT ARCHITECTURE

**Other books by or including the writing of Bette Jones Hammel**

*100 Places Plus 1: An Unofficial Architectural Survey of Favorite Minnesota Sites,* 1996

*From Bauhaus to Bowties: HGA Celebrates 35 Years,* 1989

*Legendary Homes* of *Lake Minnetonka,* 2010

*Legendary Homes of the Minneapolis Lakes,* 2012

*The Great Houses of Summit Avenue and the Hill District,* 2013

# WILD ABOUT ARCHITECTURE

Bette Hammel

Big Picture Press, Minneapolis

Published by Big Picture Press, LLC
Karen Melvin
kmelvinphoto@comcast.net

Cover photo by Christian Öser: City of Arts and Sciences, Valencia, Spain

Book design by Dorie McClelland, springbookdesign.com
Copyediting by E.B. Green Editorial, Saint Paul

International Standard Book Number: 978-0-9892627-1-2

Library of Congress Control Number: 2015950112

Library of Congress Cataloging-in-publication Data

Hammel, Bette, 1925-
Wild About Architecture / Bette Hammel
1. Architecture/Individual Architects and Firms/Essays
2. Biography/Personal Memoirs
3. Architecture/Buildings/General

Manufactured in the United States.
10 9 8 7 6 5 4 3 2 1

To Susan, my loving daughter and best friend

# Contents

## Part II: Becoming a Professional Architectural Journalist

## Part III: Encounters and Travels

# Preface

In tackling this retrospective, I found that the most difficult problem was selecting from among the hundreds of articles I've written during the past 30 years. My choice is based on whether particular buildings have made a significant impact on their communities and whether the architecture leaves a lasting impression. Also I have asked whether the work of the particular architect stands out from the crowd.

I wound up starting with 16 stories originally published in *Architecture Minnesota, Mpls.St.Paul, Skyway News, Architectural Record* (New York City), and the AIA Minnesota book *100 Places Plus 1: An Unofficial Architectural Survey of Favorite Minnesota Sites* (1996). The reader will find that I have personalized the stories here, placing myself in the interviews, scenes, and descriptions and providing updates. The chapter headings reflect the date of publication.

Architects may especially enjoy the first story, "Four Cabins," relating how four award-winning but competing modernists designed four distinctive family cabins on one lakeshore site in northern Wisconsin. Other stories cover various Twin Cities buildings such as the Ordway Music Theatre, four new towers of the 1990s, the Minneapolis Federal Building and U.S. Courthouse, the Science Museum of Minnesota, Maya Lin's wet installation for AEF (Ameriprise), and the Saint Paul Hotel. Stories about two Twin Cities churches and three residences include those on the James J. Hill House, the Davis/Winton/Nelson House by Philip Johnson, and the little Winton Guest House by Frank Gehry.

In Part III, I focus on my encounters with "starchitects," then describe travel and adventures after my husband's death to see landmark architecture including the pyramids, the lost city of Petra, and historic sites in London, Paris, Barcelona, Dubrovnik, and Istanbul. I entered on some of those adventures with writing assignments, the results of which were subsequently published. Others are new stories based on my travel journals, which provided material about works by architects such as Santiago Calatrava.

Talk about adventure! My favorite is one of the last in the book, featuring six Minnesota blondes sailing on the Adriatic via rental yacht to Dubrovnik, shortly after the Bosnian War. Yes, I handled the jib. And I sold my story to *Architectural Record.*

Many people travel the world visiting museums, cathedrals, landscapes, plazas, historic towns, famous boulevards, theaters, and more. Why not do the same in your own state? If you do, you will realize how much the architecture of our homes, business towers, museums, theaters, churches, colleges, and libraries adds to the quality of our lives.

Many, many thanks to all my architect friends—the reason I've focused on architecture through most of my writing career.

# Introduction

How did I, a former advertising copywriter, get so mixed up with architecture?

After graduating from the University of Minnesota in 1947, I began a communications career that evolved from radio writing and broadcasting to ad-agency TV production and copywriting to freelance public relations. I was the hard-working, single mom of a daughter, Susan, age four, in 1970, when both my personal and professional lives abruptly changed.

I met and married Dick Hammel, father of two adult children—Stephen and Anne. He was also the well-known architect and cofounder of Hammel Green and Abrahamson (HGA) Architects and Engineers. From Dick I began to learn about another creative profession.

I was nervous the first time Dick took me to a staff party to meet his colleagues. What would we have in common? How would I fit in? Very quickly I realized these people were creative folks with a great spirit of fun and energy, much like the ad-agency group I had just left. I could find a new home in the world of architecture.

For Dick Hammel, architecture was life, and he never stopped drawing—at the office, at home in the evenings, on summer vacations at Madeline Island, and on trips abroad. His colleagues remember that in first meetings with clients, he drew upside down to convince them to hire the firm.

He was also known for his dry wit. Dan Avchen, CEO of HGA for 19 years, recalled: "One Friday we were coming back from lunch and found the following note posted on the bulletin board: 'At 1:30 today a cannonball was shot off down the length of the drafting room. No one was injured.—R. F. Hammel.'"

In 1982, *TIME* magazine interviewed Dick about his national AIA award–winning design for the Colonial Church of Edina. He said, "Architecture is wonderful work because something other than dollars is valued. We are designing for the celebration of human life."

This is still true.

Richard Hammel, managing the office from his desk

# Part I: Early Freelancing

Four Award-winning Modernists: (l-r, top) Bruce Abrahamson and James Stageberg, (bottom) Leonard Parker and John Rauma

# 1 Four Cabins 1970

Early in our marriage (in 1970), Dick Hammel told me that his partner, Bruce Abrahamson, was excited about a unique venture "up north." Abrahamson had teamed up with Leonard Parker, John Rauma, and James Stageberg to build separate but compatible family cabins on one Wisconsin lakeshore site.

"What? Those competitors are actually working together?" I exclaimed.

"Not exactly," said Dick, "but they started with the same design concept—a simple cube."

Years later I unearthed a story originally published in the Fall/Winter 1976 issue of *Building Manual* and another in the September 1982 issue of *Architecture Minnesota.* My story draws from the earlier articles and recent interviews with the architects' families:

In the late 1960s, four young modernists—Bruce Abrahamson, Leonard Parker, John Rauma, and James Stageberg—were known as hotshot architects in Minnesota. Abrahamson was professorial, delightful and fun. Parker was a quick-witted, sharp, gifted teacher. Rauma, with Finnish reserve, was wise and nonjudgmental. Stageberg was warm, generous, and passionate about architecture. As friends and fierce competitors, the four architects often gathered to swap stories and complain about the low fees they were getting.

"I sure wish I had a cabin up north to get away once in a while," said Stageberg.

They all agreed but acknowledged, "We're too poor."

"Well, why don't we buy a piece of property together? That way we can pool our money," said ever-the-optimist Abrahamson.

Each man realized that together they could use their art to create a cohesive modernist community—they should go for it.

As a first step the architects contacted a real estate agent in the area of Hayward, Wisconsin. That fell through . . . but ultimately the same agent, who had come to know the four guys well, offered his own property for sale on a great lakefront site—if, and *only* if, they designed a cabin for him, too. The four promptly agreed.

The property was on the Eau Claire chain of lakes near Barnes, Wisconsin. The architects piled their families, complete with 17 children, into four cars and took off to find it. Nestled on the crest of a hill in a Wisconsin forest overlooking a crystal-clear lake connected to a lower lake of about the same size, it was a perfect spot for growing families. The property had once contained the Five Pines Resort, some years earlier destroyed by a forest fire.

Excited about the property, which had 500 feet of shoreline, the four men sat down at dinner to discuss what they might do.

Parker jokingly asked, "What's your cabin going to look like, Bruce?"

Promptly, each of the four started drawing on his paper napkin, then a customary way to entice a new client. It turned out that each architect had sketched a 45-degree triangle to represent his cabin section. They agreed on the criteria for design based on a simple wedge/cube. The designs evolved in accordance with each one's particular style.

The four architects decided to use the same materials, including Pella sliding glass doors as the module for the cabins' dimensions, and 1 x 6 cedar boards for the exteriors and interiors,

Leonard Parker's cabin

This space was Stageberg's favorite place to work at his cabin.

The dramatic exterior of Bruce Abrahamson's cabin

including cabinetry and built-ins. There would be no private docks. It made more sense to build one big common dock. (Ultimately the common dock collapsed so many times that it became a standing joke. It seems they forgot to hire an engineer.)

The four cabins were to be built in a line from north to south, each facing west and with plenty of space between them. Jim Stageberg, who with six children had the biggest family, said he needed the site at the far north end of the property. He designed a flat roof over three stories for the greatest amount of usable cubic footage. That allowed a leftover volume over the main floor to bring in the light. The kitchen was tucked under the second floor with dining on the other end of the room.

The Stageberg cabin today looks like a great cedar box with punched-out windows for views. Of its flat roof, Stageberg said, "I tried working with the wedge, but everything I did at that time had a flat roof on it." And ultimately, no one objected.

Leonard Parker took advantage of the wedge form. In his case the form is extravagant, with a high, sloping roof on one side. On the other side is a small pyramid allowing light to enter above an interior spiral stairway and a cutout section at the entrance made into an open porch. For fun, he added a crow's nest at the highest point, allowing great views of the lake. Upon arrival the Parker family always hung a huge orange Japanese-dragon kite above the deck. Parker deliberately left holes in the deck for shade trees.

Of living in such proximity to his architect friends, Parker noted: "The four of us were often competing for the same job, so we'd tease each other to see how much the other guy would tell you about what he was doing."

Bruce Abrahamson always liked towers, so his cabin was sited on a steep slope, perched on telephone-pole piers. A sauna tucks below a big triangular deck. The cabin is one floor with a spiral stair leading to three double beds in a cozy loft overlooking the fireplace below. Its striking roof form pitches two triangular surfaces against each other to form a valley.

According to Victoria Abrahamson, Bruce said, "We built it for only $25,000." But he noted, "I doubt that in the end we really saved any money by building together, but it was easier for the builder and very satisfying for us."

John Rauma stayed with a simple cube, upstairs and down. John and his wife, Wanda, pored over the drawings together before finalizing their decisions. The roof features a small shed-roofed extension creating space for a circular stairway that leads to a sleeping loft with built-in bunks. The Raumas painted their white window trim black, inspired by the soft grey weathering of the cedar.

John Rauma noted: "A lot of our trees are aspen and poplar. When their leaves pivot on the stem, we hear a rustling sound. This can be very pleasing."

The visitor approaching this unique community of four visually compatible cabins gets a sense of looking at "tree houses." Sure enough, the architects felt that by elevating the cabins they would do the least damage to the environment. But one problem developed as a result—some of their pipes froze. They wrapped the pipes with insulation—or installed saunas around the pipes.

The same builder, a friendly chap the architects dubbed "Chet the Builder," constructed all four cabins. In addition, the four men kept their promise to their real estate agent, designing a cabin for him of cube shape and similar materials. Former Cargill executive Bill Pearce and his wife, Barbara A. (Smith) Pearce, own it now.

The cedar cladding of the cabins, built in 1970 and 1971, has weathered gray, and cedar shakes have replaced all of the roofs. But the structures are still very much in use by the architects' families. Of the four, only John Rauma sold his cabin. The adult children of two of the original owners and one widow with grandchildren regularly make use of the other three. The community is known as the "Windrose Five."

In 1972, the four architects were pleased to win a Minnesota AIA honor award for their outstanding example of architectural cooperation. Today all four of the dedicated fun-loving architects are deceased. In his time, each one—Leonard Parker in 1986, James Stageberg in 1991, Bruce Abrahamson in 1998, and John Rauma in 2000—was named an AIA Minnesota Gold Medalist.

This story draws from "Four Architects Pool Their Talents" (no author given) published in *Building Manual* (a *House Beautiful* Special Publication, 1975–76) and from "Four Cabins Fit Four Families" (no author given) in the September 1982 issue of *Architecture Minnesota.*

I learned of the project's beginnings from Victoria Dyer (Mrs. Bruce A.) Abrahamson, Wanda McIntire (Mrs. John) Rauma, and other family members who are now practicing architects—Jane Stageberg of Bade Stageberg Cox (New York City) and Aaron Parker of Metropeligo (Minneapolis).

Dick Hammel and I visited each of these wonderful cabins during their early years.

# 2 Stone Arch Bridge 1991

In the 1970s and 1980s years of freelancing during my married life (I was also bringing up my daughter, Susan), I occasionally landed a good story assignment from a local editor. The headline of one story read: "A Walk across the Stone Arch Bridge." The year? 1981. No one was allowed to cross the historic structure because of safety concerns.

On a wet and blustery day in late October, I was granted permission to cross the Stone Arch Bridge on foot, accompanied by longtime Minneapolis Park and Recreation Board member and former president Patricia (Pat) Hillmeyer and the board's landscape architect, Bob Madison. Both expressed hope for the near future that the bridge might be remodeled and reinforced to ensure complete safety for pedestrians and bikers.

They had grand visions, too: Hillmeyer, whose mission had always been redevelopment of the riverfront, visualized the old milling towers as apartments. Perhaps there would be a museum to present the history of the Falls of Saint Anthony . . . and archeologists would reveal some of the inner workings of the tailraces that had brought in the waterpower that made Minneapolis the milling capital of the world. Madison thought a park might be built on the lower embankment.

Stone Arch Bridge: Built in 1883, rebuilt for pedestrian safety in 1994

As we gazed at the swirling force of the falls, I gasped at its tremendous power. The entire history of the city was laid out before me—the river, the parklands on either side, the aging flour mills, and the skyline of modern Minneapolis. This panorama unfolds before anyone standing on the 150-year-old railroad, just where it curves around the locks.

Obviously, funding was crucial to accomplishing their visions. Hennepin County had bought the bridge (built in 1883) three years earlier. Now the board was waiting for the county, acting as Regional Railroad Authority, to approve monies to make the structure safe for pedestrians and bikers. Madison said that would take three major steps: Resurfacing the pathway (at that time still railroad bedrock), adding new railings, and providing modern lighting.

Other groups, including the Saint Anthony Falls Heritage Preservation Board and the Minnesota Historical Society, were interested in the Stone Arch Bridge, too. And in 1989 the Hennepin County Regional Railroad Authority bought the bridge. Soon renovation began. Later the Minnesota Department of Transportation (MNDOT) acquired ownership. In 1994 the Stone Arch Bridge opened to the public as a pedestrian walkway/biking path.

The grander vision of my two bridge companions became real upon the subsequent creation of the Mill City Museum, the conversion of other old mills to residential apartments, and the establishment of an archaeological park along the river. Today thousands of local enthusiasts and tourists walk, run, jog, and bike safely across the old bridge, stopping to admire the Falls of Saint Anthony, still a symbol of the city's power.

This story draws from my article "A Walk across the Stone Arch Bridge," published in the October 31, 1991, issue of *Skyway News.*

# 3 Saint Paul Hotel 1982

In 1982, I landed another intriguing writing assignment. Brian Anderson, since-deceased editor of *Mpls.St.Paul* magazine, who knew I was "a Saint Paul girl," called and asked me to do an article about the renovation of the Saint Paul Hotel. It was a juicy assignment as my uncle was the retired general manager of the hotel, and he had invited my family there many times. I knew the Saint Paul had been at the center of action in the city from the time of its opening in 1910.

Recalling some of the rollicking times I had seen there in the 1940s and '50s, I wrote about the rowdy Klondike Kate in the ballroom, the Hook'em Cows (a basketball team) riding into the lobby on horses during Winter Carnival, the big shots making deals in the Gopher Grill, carved ice and huge bouquets in the dining room, the first-in-the-Midwest Sunday smorgasbord, dance bands broadcast by KSTP radio from the downstairs Casino Ballroom from 1928, and the city's elite dressed to the hilt. The hotel was like a theater set.

The hotel's original architects—of local firm Reed & Stem, which went on to design New York's Grand Central Terminal—played up elegance in the Italian Renaissance style of the hotel, rising to 12 stories clad in brick and terracotta tile and opening in 1910. Given its architecture, mahogany furniture, linens woven in Ireland, and huge crystal chandeliers, hotelmen called it "the best hotel in the West."

Despite periods of remodeling, the hotel fell into decline and closed in 1979. It was a major blow to the city. Four years later, new owners took possession. By 1981, city leaders called for a major renovation. Owner of Jefferson Bus Lines Louis Zelle, heading a new financial team for the city, announced that it wanted the hotel to blossom as an elegant facility again and had hired HGA as chief designer, with interior design to be done by Tom Lee Ltd., New York. Crews of workers thoroughly cleaned and repaired the mellow brick and white exterior and gutted the interior. Bruce Abrahamson and Dan Avchen, principal architects, said there was nothing left to restore; they wanted to capture the Old World feeling the hotel had earlier.

The architects knew that Tom Lee's wife, Sarah Tomerlin Lee, had done beautiful restorations of such grand hotels as Willard Intercontinental of Washington, D.C., Helmsley Palace in New York, and others, and they asked her to join the team. When she arrived, Dick Hammel asked me to take her around the Twin Cities to shop for art and elegant objects.

Meeting Sarah Lee was my lucky day. She was a captivating older woman, always wearing her pearls and a fashionable navy-blue dress with cape and matching hat. She spilled over with stories of her days as an editor of *Vogue* and *Harper's Bazaar* and of matching wits with *New Yorker* columnist Brendan Gill. She and I got on famously while I drove her to Twin City art galleries and museums, introducing her to antique dealers and shops. In later years, we lunched together in her favorite New York clubs. (Sarah Tomerlin Lee died in 2000, leaving a long legacy in the fashion, retail, and interior design industries.)

As interior designer for the restoration, Sara Lee set about redecorating all the Saint Paul Hotel rooms, selecting new artwork for public spaces, insisting on a more glamorous lobby with

Saint Paul Hotel: First major remodeling, 1981

fireplace, and installing a sparkling chandelier leading downstairs to her Scandinavian-style breakfast room in blue and yellow.

One of the architects' major improvements in the 1982 renovation was reestablishment of the hotel's main entrance from Saint Peter Street to Market Street to face the greenery of Rice Park. Guests now arrive via a circular drive to be greeted with valet parking. Flower gardens line the drive. The Saint Paul reopened to acclaim in mid-December 1983, and the magic returned.

In 1990, architect Dan Avchen was called back to design a new hotel restaurant, facing the park across the street. The Saint Paul Hotel Grill has since become one of the most popular restaurants in the Twin Cities. The hotel has retained its elegance and is now ranked a four-star establishment. It is a historic landmark vital to the city.

This story draws from my article "The Saint Paul Comes Back in a New Package," published in the September 1982 issue of *Mpls.St.Paul.*

# 4 Ordway Music Theatre 1985

In 1984 came one of my most exciting assignments yet—from Group Seven Graphics—to write and produce the opening program magazine for the forthcoming Ordway Music Theatre. This is the basic story, with updates:

In my first conversations with the lauded Bostonian architect Ben Thompson, I realized how well he understood the urban environment and the business of theater. In describing his design for the Ordway, Thompson said, "The design of this theater, like music, is at once intimate, then surrounding, classical and yet irregular. It's a rhythmic shape."

The since-deceased architect and his firm, Benjamin Thompson & Associates (BTA Cambridge) is widely recognized for the ability to design festive urban structures such as for the Boston waterfront, Faneuil Hall Marketplace, Harborplace on the Baltimore waterfront, and South Street Seaport in New York. As a native Saint Paulite, Thompson's selection for design of the Ordway was not exactly unexpected, and I had a private hunch the "good old boys of Saint Paul," had a lot to do with it.

Interviewing Thompson further, I found he was still proud of his hometown but felt that the city had missed an opportunity to open itself to the Mississippi River, its greatest natural asset.

ORDWAY
THE
PIRATES
PENZANCE

Ordway Center for the Performing Arts, 2015: The Ordway Concert Hall, seating an audience of 1,100, replaced the smaller McKnight Theatre, improving on its acoustics.

The architect also knew there was great need for a new cultural amenity in the city.

When the old Saint Paul Civic Auditorium theater was closed due to structural deterioration in 1980, the city was left without a downtown performance hall. A hastily formed committee turned to Sally Ordway Irvine for support. Together they toured other facilities and invited a local architect to sketch a theater for drama.

Out of the blue, Ordway Irvine (later the theater's vice president) said, "I want a theater for *all* the performing arts.

Advisor Henry Blodgett, later the theater's vice president, remembered, "Everyone turned white!" He suggested asking an old school chum, Ben Thompson, for ideas. Within a year, they had a site right on the Rice Park square.

Funding the Ordway Music Theatre was another question. Suddenly and dramatically, the Ordway family, led by Sally Ordway Irvine, presented the community with a challenge. She committed to paying for the plans for the new venue and proposed that she and members of her family put together about $15 million, to be matched by the Saint Paul/Minneapolis community. Other civic leaders, corporations, and foundations led a successful capital fund drive accompanied by a $10 million loan from the McKnight Foundation. An old friend and neighbor of Ben Thompson, Ordway Irvine was well pleased with the result.

Sally Ordway Irvine was a spunky fun-loving woman, known for her love of life and especially the theater. When I interviewed her at her home, she confessed, "I always wanted to be an actress," and "I used to sneak in after school at the stage door of the Saint Paul Civic Auditorium theater." Her grandmother Jessie (Mrs. Lucius) P. Ordway and her father, John Pond Ordway, who helped launch what became the 3M Company, loved opera. It was only natural that Sally Ordway Irvine, Ben Thompson, and others tour London, Rome, Vienna, and Paris to check out the attributes of Old World opera houses.

Thompson was determined to build a romantic ambience into the new venue. Knowing that even the entrance of the audience to the theater is a performance, he and his team designed a sweeping spiral staircase—the Grand Stair—leading to the mezzanine and the Grand Foyer. There theatergoers mingle, promenade, enjoy liquid refreshment, and admire the view of Rice Park glittering with lights, the city skyline, and the river beyond. In many ways the Ordway was designed as much for its patrons as for its performers. It provides ample opportunity to see and be seen.

Ordway's main hall is a classical horseshoe, as in the grand tradition of European opera houses, with three shallow curving balconies ending in tiers of boxes close to the stage.

Externally, the challenge for the design team was to produce a multipurpose hall that could serve as a concert hall as well as an opera house so that the Minnesota Opera Company, the Saint Paul Chamber Orchestra, the Schubert Club, and occasionally the Minnesota Orchestra could find a home there.

Inside and out, the architecture of the Ordway is dramatic. Seen from Rice Park, it is a glistening prism of copper and glass. At night it is aglow with movement.

"We designed a kind of faceted front that steps back and forth so that its reflections . . . capture images of the classic buildings in the square," said Thompson.

In contrast to the sharply defined sculptural shape of the building is the warmth of the copper roof and the handmade exterior red brick from a kiln in New Hampshire.

For 30 years the Ordway Music Theatre served the larger community well. It brought a long-missing heartbeat back to the center of Saint Paul. With a few architectural changes during that period, the Ordway came to host Broadway musical shows on its stage.

In February 2015 the Ordway—redubbed the Ordway Center for the Performing Arts—stood poised on an even brighter future. Its new Concert Hall expands on and replaces the

Ordway Concert Hall
Original Sketch by Tim Carl, FAIA

The architect's rendering of the Ordway Concert Hall for the Saint Paul Chamber Orchestra, 2015

McKnight Theatre of the original building but is designed especially for the Saint Paul Chamber Orchestra, which as a smaller ensemble was not fully accommodated by the acoustics of the original hall.

According to architect Tim Carl, CEO of HGA, acoustics presented only the first problem he had to solve. The resulting Ordway Concert Hall design features a dramatic mahogany-stained ceiling crafted of extensive oak dolems undulating from the stage to the third balcony. Thanks to new acoustical technology, this gives the musicians the sound they have wanted. Another challenge, Carl said, was matching the original copper and glass-faceted façade in the Ordway extension.

Today Twin Citians still love the "grand entry" feeling of the Ordway, its great views, comfortable seating, three levels, and especially its classical ambience. Ben Thompson once, and Tim Carl again, created a music theater with a future.

This story draws from the program magazine I prepared for the opening of the Ordway on January 1, 1985.

# 5 Paris 1985

From the time my husband Dick Hammel was a boy dreaming about architecture, he longed to see Mont Saint-Michel, the mystical church rising from a high rocky islet in the Atlantic. Location: Normandy, France. With the help of a good travel agent, he planned a three-week vacation with our family in 1985, including certain luxuries such as Relais & Châteaux reservations across the Loire Valley. His goal was to see the great cathedrals and other landmark architecture of Paris and to discover the château country.

We all—our two daughters, especially—were excited about the trip. Susan had been traveling through Europe on an after-college plan; her older stepsister, Anne, a choreographer and alternative therapist, was living in New York. They instantly made plans to join us at the Hotel Mayfair Paris for a week together in France.

Dick and I flew to Paris on August 31, picked up our car, and clutching our map, drove into the city to find the Mayfair. There hanging out on the first-floor balcony were two laughing girls, one blond, the other brunette, waving madly and shouting, "Dad!" The two rumpled travelers had just transferred from an overnight at a Paris fleabag and were luxuriating in the elegant hotel. We reunited with joyful hugs and mapped out our plans:

Members of the family—Anne, Susan, Dick, and Bette—
met in Paris to begin a tour of the Loire Valley.

a couple of days in Paris, then the château tour and Mont Saint-Michel to round out the week.

The next morning we headed out, Susan at the wheel (she was the only one who spoke French.) Crossing the Place de la Concorde required all her grit. There were no lanes, no stops, just a whirl of traffic from all directions! Susan drove around the circle twice, then shot down the Champs Élysées, under and around the Arc de Triomphe, looking for Boulevard Périphérique. Uncertain of where to turn, she rolled down the window and shouted for directions from the nearest driver. He answered with a smile, and soon we were headed for Chartres.

The 11th-century hillside Chartres Cathedral was a must for Dick, who remarked at first glimpse, "It looks a lot more worn than I expected." I had packed a French picnic of bread, cheese, and wine, which we ate in the sun, gazing up at the cathedral's vertical gothic façade. Then, entering the darkened cathedral, we stood marveling at the stunning stained-blue-glass windows. No wonder it took so long to build this landmark!

Our first morning spent in Paris naturally meant a visit to another famed cathedral—Notre Dame. Again, Dick thought it was more worn than expected, but we were moved by its magnificent rose windows and its site on the Île de la Cité: the huge plaza, the flying buttresses, the gargoyles used as rainspouts, the gardens, and the crushed limestone paths along the River Seine. Dick was impressed by the solid round columns that supported the church inside.

In the afternoon we visited the Louvre and its treasures, rode the Paris Metro, and toured another church, the Sacré-Coeur, a white limestone, Roman-looking church with huge dome and arches. Our day ended with a trip down the Seine by barge, offering a different vista of the magical city.

Piling into the car on our third day, the family enjoyed the green rolling countryside as the car passed through old stone-clad villages. Soon after the road narrowed, we found our first Relais hotel, the Château de Teildras, nestled in a pastoral setting of blooming rose gardens and dahlias. The château was built of limestone and with all three stories spanned by enormous oak and walnut beams. Its cuisine was outstanding and its beds so comfortable, we hated to leave.

The small city of Dinard in Brittany was our next destination. Even in the poorest streets of the French villages we passed through, the flowers—bright pink geraniums, yellow marigolds, and red and pink roses—grew in abundance. Dinard, though touristy, was a pretty town perched high above a valley. Its streets were winding and its buildings were of dark-brown stone.

We soon found our hotel, the Villa Reine Hortense, and immediately fell in love with the romantic old place and its main salon, the Marie Antoinette. Our rooms overlooked La Mare, and when I looked down to the beach festooned with colorful beach umbrella chairs. it reminded me of the scenes in the children's book *Babar*. I could just visualize Celeste, the mother elephant, and her babies walking towards their umbrella.

For dinner in the town, we walked to Hotel de l'Atelier, for one of the most delicious meals yet. We gulped fresh oysters, then a heavenly *fleur aux moules* (mussels), then strips of *poulet* set into a rosette and *truite au rouge*. The two-and-a-half-hour dinner cost us only about $40.

On the beach that afternoon I happened to meet a French teenager and his mother. The boy, spotting me as an American, wanted to try out his English, and he succeeded. I learned they were a sailing family who often vacationed there from Paris. His mother promptly invited us for 7 PM aperitifs. Later, Dick and I took a walk along the promontories overlooking the sea and realized the area was a yachting center. The scene immediately reminded Dick of his own sailboat-racing schedule with the Minnetonka Yacht Club back home.

Meanwhile, as Dick and Anne went for a walk, Susan and I suddenly realized it was time to visit our new French friends. We found their apartment up the cliff next to a beautiful burgundy and white Victorian house. The boy's mother and her two pretty daughters served us aperitifs and snacks. The 16-year-old Hubert kept talking to me in English, showing me pictures of his American visit to Ohio. I realized he wanted to come to America again, so I invited him to visit our home and gave him our address. Two years later he did come to visit us. It was great fun to share our American home with a young Frenchman.

Dick Hammel, gazing at Mont Saint-Michel

The next day was our long-awaited pilgrimage to Mont Saint-Michel. It was a rainy, misty day, somehow perfect for viewing the abbey. The tide—the highest in Europe—was out that morning, and we easily walked to the island on the sand. What an amazing sight it was—the church rising to the heavens from the sea.

We climbed narrow winding steps so as to start our tour from the top. Once there, we learned about the Romanesque portions of the church, then the gothic section, at which the guide described the lives of the monks. The place seemed impenetrable.

By 1 PM, we had descended to the restaurant on Mont Saint-Michel, famous for its omelets. Cooked over an open fire by two men using copper bowls and long-handled pans, the puffy omelets were scrumptious.

Dick thought the winding street, varying from a one to eight feet and leading up to the abbey, was marvelous. The buildings were two or three stories high. The abbey became more human when we learned it was planned as a place for monks to meditate (in the cloister), and for pilgrims, royalty, and others to eat, work, and sleep. All this had been woven around the pinnacle of rock, the church at its peak.

Our next château—Relais Château d'Audrieu—was in the countryside of Caen. It was a grand place with a huge forecourt of gravel, a lovely garden, and fruit trees. After our stay there, we reluctantly bid our girls good-bye as they departed for home from the airport at Caen.

We resumed driving through Brittany, admiring the architecture of *Bretagne* houses. All of it seemed built in traditional house shapes of local stone with matching roofs. We drove the side roads, enjoying the small villages, finding good restaurants everywhere and seaside hotels where I could swim while Dick napped. I was delighted with Brittany, a tiny eastern section of France along the Atlantic, with its own special architecture, cuisine, and hospitality.

Our next destination was the Normandy beaches, which we both wanted to see. Dick had been a naval officer in the Pacific, but like most Americans, we had lost friends in the crucial D-Day battle in Normandy during World War II. In Arromanches, we visited the museum that overlooks the scene of the historic landing. Inside we learned of the preparations, the floating piers, the concrete walls, and more.

A little farther up the coast, we toured in silence the American cemetery, unforgettable with its hundreds of white crosses marching across the green lawn overlooking a peaceful coastline.

Back in the Loire Valley, we decided that seeing two particular châteaux was a must. First was the "thrill of thrills," the famous Château de Chenonceau, which properly impressed us for the way

Bette in the rose garden of Château de Chenonceau

it stretches across the River Cher in a stone extension. The splendid approach is bordered by huge plane trees. Off to the right were the beautiful Catherine de Médicis formal gardens, all pink petunias, rose trees, and carefully trimmed green hedges. I thought the gardens were more impressive than the interior château.

Next we headed south to see the Château de Chambord. It was huge in its storybook setting complete with ruins, lacy towers, tall chimneys, and cone-shaped, slate roofs. This château of pink and white brick (for a change), surrounded by acres of parkland, had served as a hunting capital for royalty.

On our return to Paris, we drove through the valley of the Marne, where much of World War I was fought, then headed for champagne country. After passing row upon row of green grapes, we noticed a giant atomic-energy plant and cooling tower on the horizon; 90 percent of France was then nuclear-powered. Dick wanted to see the plant up close, but we wound up in a new suburb instead. There he spotted a contemporary elementary school worth some photography.

The next day it was off to Reims, to see the renowned cathedral there, another long-awaited visit for Dick. Reims was heavily damaged during both wars, and we noticed particularly the many modern buildings on its outskirts.

As we approached the cathedral, Dick exclaimed over the scale of the façades and noticed that the two towers, though symmetrical, are different in their decoration. The faces, statues, gargoyles, eagles, archers, boars, and stone tracery on the towers comprise a plethora of detail.

From the south side, we could see right through the church's immense windows. The giant rose window of reds above the smaller rose window of deep blue came alive as, unexpectedly, we heard a choir beginning to sing in Latin. It was almost like a voice from heaven. Lots of restoration was still going on around the transept and the north towers, where huge scaffolding stood. The most striking windows in the choir loft are contemporary stained glass created by Marc Chagall in 1974 in astonishingly bright blues, greens, and violets. I was transfixed. Dick found the Reims Cathedral one of the most moving experiences of our entire trip.

Returning to Paris for the last three days of our sojourn, we turned in the car and via cab found the Hotel Ferrandi in Montparnasse. After a brief lunch, we walked to the Eiffel Tower via the UNESCO Headquarters, which as Dick pointed out, was a more contemporary structure, designed by Marcel Breuer (architect of the Abbey Church of Saint John the Baptist) in the 1950s. Outside and in were sculptures by Alexander Calder and Henry Moore, frescoes by Pablo Picasso, Joan Miró, and others, and a Japanese sculpture garden by Isamu Noguchi. Concrete, steel, and glass completed the complex of buildings.

We took a two-mile walk, admiring the flowers of the Jardin des Tuileries on our way to the Eiffel Tower. It was crowded, but the climb to the top was worth it. That visit to the tower was a great way to say good-bye to Paris. Dick said the city looked all white, dazzling in the late-afternoon September sun. We could see the old and the new of Paris, the broad Seine, its handsome boulevards, arched bridges, and many barges dividing the city in half.

What a magnificent city! I had seen it earlier, but this was the best. As Dick noted, "This city is romantic by design—there are not many straight lines . . . And the mansard-roofed buildings that house so many Parisians are curving and create shadows. They are so uniform in style with their wrought-iron balconies and five to six stories, their distinctive doors and inner courtyards. I can see why it takes people living right in the heart of a city to make a city great."

Exploring France was Dick Hammel's last major trip.

This story draws from my travel journal of that family trip.

# 6 Transitions 1986–1989

On November 18, 1986, the sky fell in. Dick Hammel died suddenly at University Hospital in Minneapolis at the age of 63. The funeral was held at Colonial Church of Edina, where Dick had worked on for seven years with the Rev. Dr. Arthur Rouner, who officiated that day. The church was packed.

A year later, a colonial-style covered bridge leading to the rear entry of the building, designed by Dick's colleague Ted Butler, was dedicated in Dick's memory. I was still devastated, but I knew that working would help me, particularly as I was a newly single mom. I learned that HGA would be celebrating its 35th anniversary the next year, and I asked Dick's partners whether I could write something for the occasion. They not only agreed but also decided the firm should produce a book about its history—and that I should write it. Researching and writing that book was a challenge and a broad and deep learning experience.

Three years later, thanks to the insight of Dick's founding partner, Curt Green, and with help from HGA public relations staff, we produced *From Bauhaus to Bowties: HGA Celebrates 35 Years,* in 1989. The company sent it to architectural libraries across the country.

I had lost Dick, and I did not want to lose the world of architecture too. Thanks to my interviews of a host of architects, engineers, and landscape and interior designers, the book project had taught me the language of architecture. I was hooked on the subject and determined to continue writing about it. In fact, I would *concentrate* on architectural writing to better inform the public of the importance of architecture in our lives.

In essence, I became an advocate for all architects.

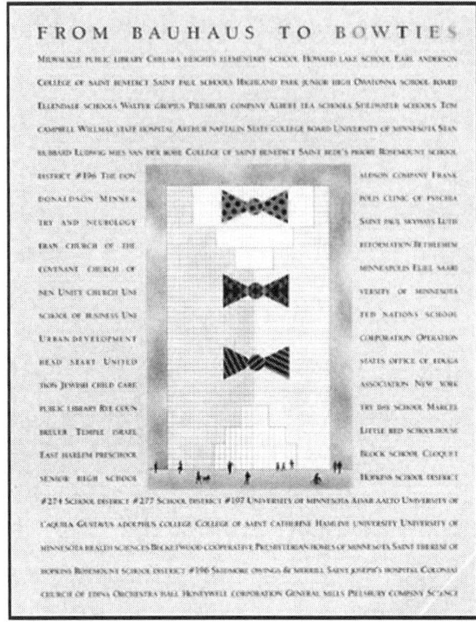


HGA's 35th anniversary history, *From Bauhaus to Bowties*, by Bette Hammel, 1989

Dick and Bette Hammel dressed formally to attend the Symphony Ball, an annual event benefiting the Minnesota Orchestra.

Richard Hammel, the love of my life, died on November 18, 1986, at age 63.

# Part II: Becoming a Professional Architectural Journalist

# 7 New York 1988

While finishing the HGA history, I attended the 1988 AIA National Convention in New York City. Three events stood out: a ship-to-shore cruise around Manhattan led by Brendan Gill, erudite architecture critic for *The New Yorker*; a tour of the IBM Headquarters (590 Madison) with its architect, Edward Larrabee Barnes; and best of all, a visit to the apartment home of Kohn Pedersen Fox (KPF) founder Bill Pedersen, on Central Park West.

"At this very moment, New York is being destroyed by overbuilding by unscrupulous developers," declared Brendan Gill. "This city is out of control . . . It's thrilling and dreadful, the most difficult of all cities to live in yet the one we take great joy in living here." As we cruised, it was obvious to those of us on board how much Gill loved his city yet despaired of the proliferation of towers there.

Known for his caustic wit, Gill relished taking several pokes at certain establishment architects: "Some of our prominent prima donnas are about to have the curtain rung down on them. Farewell to the Philip Johnsons, I. M. Peis, Kevin Roches . . . Welcome all you young students. Change is necessary."

As we rounded the tip of lower Manhattan, Gill continued his merciless critique. "We've really had a series of catastrophes here, including the Twin Towers of the World Trade Center.

Our tour via ferryboat around the island of Manhattan, led by Brenden Gill of *The New Yorker*, was a rare treat at the 1988 national AIA convention.

Fortunately the slab-type skyscraper is fading out of favor." (Brendan Gill died in 1998, before the 9/11 disaster.)

Then as the ship passed Battery Park, Gill couldn't help himself: "Pelli's buildings strike a sort of Mussolini-like note. You pat these columns and they go bang, bang." (The 9/11 disaster took care of these.)

Gill saved his more positive remarks for the favorites of the 19th century near the historic financial district—the U.S. Custom House by Cass Gilbert, the Manhattan Municipal Building by McKim Mead & White, and the city's first skyscraper, the Woolworth Building, also by Gilbert.

As we cruised up the East River (really a canal), Gill pointed out his favorite residential buildings of the 1920s—Beekman Place where Irving Berlin lived, Sutton Place South where I. M. Pei lived, and another, newer building in which Gloria Vanderbilt resided. Gill directed his parting words to young architects: "Godspeed in the middle of the muddle yet to come."

In contrast, the debonair Edward Larrabee Barnes (principal architect for the Walker Art Center in Minneapolis) was gracious and obviously proud of his new IBM Headquarters and its extra setback from the street: "The very daring cantilever . . . opened the entrance at the building, which created the IBM Bamboo Garden, a sunny pleasant public space for relaxing."

The tower is clad in Canadian Atlantic dark-green granite and soars 41 floors in refined and elegant style.

The standout visit for Minnesota attendees was the visit to Bill Pedersen's apartment on Central Park West, hosted by his wife, Elizabeth Essex Pedersen. As gracious hosts, they made us feel comfortable and relaxed. Harrison Fraker, then dean of the University of Minnesota School of Architecture (now College of Design), commented on Bill's design for his home: "It's a kind of art deco or modern, a synthesis of a lot of the motifs KPF used in the Lincoln Center building scaled down to residential scale."

In the years since I toured Manhattan with that group, I have tramped New York many times, realizing that the city is a living museum of architecture—the old, the new, the bold and the brilliant, the ugly and the distressing.

Fellow architecture buffs have asked me to name my favorite buildings in New York City. Here are just a few:

Number one is the Brooklyn Bridge. I'll never forget walking over the bridge a few years ago with friends. It was such an adventure, with the sounds of the traffic overhead, the horns of the ferryboats honking on the river below, and the variety of languages we heard while walking. When we reached the pinnacle of the bridge and stopped to take into view the great city before us, it was absolutely breathtaking.

The great Brooklyn Bridge, an engineering masterpiece, opened in 1883

I could see some of my favorite skyscrapers: the Chrysler Building, the Woolworth Building, the Empire State Building, and the two monumental World Trade Center towers. I had just visited the top-floor restaurant of WTC 1 (the north tower) with a friend; I remembered feeling a little squeamish about our speedy elevator ride to the top.

Favorite architectural landmarks other than those I could see from the bridge include the Guggenheim Museum by Frank Lloyd Wright, Rockefeller Center Plaza, Lincoln Center, and the Metropolitan Museum of Art.

The reader may not agree with Brendan Gill, but any even casual student of architecture will enjoy soaking up New York City's architectural gems. Look closely, and you will delight in many things you've never noticed before. I found in looking out on the harbor, for example, that Miss Liberty stands on just one foot, no doubt preparing to boot Brendan Gill's disfavored developers from Manhattan!

This story draws from my article "New York, New York," published in the June 9, 1988, issue of *Architecture Minnesota.*

# 8 My First Column 1991

Following the publication of *From Bauhaus to Bowties*, I was fretting about how to get started as an architectural journalist, and I decided early in 1991 to call on *Skyway News*. Karen and Ed Baker, both art activists, were publishers of the popular weekly then circulating in the Twin Cities. The editor, Amy Gage, soon followed by Jodie Ahern, liked the way I talked passionately about architecture and immediately said, "Go for it."

I already knew many architects—mostly men but several outstanding women: Elizabeth Close, Julie Snow, Martha Yunker, Rosemary McMonigal, Jennifer Yoos, Joan Soranno, and Rebecca Greco. All had imagination and knowledge about proportion. They paid attention to technical detail and admired landmarks abroad—timeless cathedrals, Italian villas, French châteaux, Saudi palaces, the Parthenon, and Chinese superstructures.

Most of the architects I was acquainted with knew how to draw and drew very well. Then along came the computer and the software known as CAAD (computer-aided architectural design). It was like the heavens opening. Frank Gehry, for example, became an instant superstar with models demonstrating every form of geometry.

When I started reporting about architecture in the Twin Cities, I wrote about squiggly buildings, plain buildings, towering buildings, curved buildings, new buildings, and historic buildings. I emphasized that people called *architects* designed all these structures, and I always named them.

Soon editor Gage gave me a column. I called it *Changing Skyscapes.*

# 9 Four New Towers with Plazas 1991

The appearance of four high-rise towers in downtown Minneapolis within nine months was a turning point for the architecture of the city. The time was right for my first major story. It was headlined:

Minneapolis Is Making Room for Four Stunning New Towers. But Have the Developers Remembered to Make Room for Us?

The towers, built from May 1991 through January 1992, included:

- LaSalle Plaza, 30 stories, architect Ellerbe Becket (now AECOM), Minneapolis
- AT&T Tower, 34 stories, Walsh Bishop Associates, Minneapolis
- First Bank Place, 53 stories, Pei Cobb Freed & Partners, New York
- Dain Bosworth Plaza, 40 stories, Lohan Associates, Chicago

All of these buildings were huge, featuring mostly glass façades. All were modern. And by developer agreement, each was to be accompanied by a public plaza.

Every great city needs a gathering place for the community, but for northern cities in particular, the space need not be outdoors. On an official 18th-century map of Rome, an Italian surveyor pointed out the use of interior spaces of buildings as part of the public space. In recent times, William Morrish, founding director of the University of Minnesota's Design Center for American Urban Landscape, noted, "One of the key ingredients of public space is providing a gracious entry into the building and commercial vitality."

All four of the city's new tower plazas were indoors. The question remained: Would the new buildings offer inviting space for everyone to enjoy, or would they, by design, shut out the public?

## LaSalle Plaza

Soon after the completion of LaSalle Plaza, I took a walking tour through the new building with one of the senior interior architects, Ted Davis. The complexity of the project impressed me. LaSalle Plaza was an expansive indoor shopping arcade spanning the block between Eighth and Ninth Streets and LaSalle and Hennepin Avenues with an escalator leading to a landscaped stairway space.

Principal architect Rich Varda and senior interior architect Ted Davis of Ellerbe Becket designed the 30-story tower as the firm's new corporate headquarters. At least five stories of the new tower were to house Ellerbe Becket's 500 employees. The new building incorporated the historic YMCA building (redesigned by Architectural Alliance, Minneapolis) on the Eighth Street side, the old Harriet G. Walker Building, and the State Theatre.

"It was an incredible jigsaw puzzle to figure out," said Davis.

Ellerbe Becket and Architectural Alliance jointly planned a Kasota stone and brick base wrapping around the block. What I especially liked about the exterior design was the way the architects used details symbolizing Minnesota, such as the gold-leaf wheat design at the top of the tower and on the elevator doors.

The tower's major public space is the glass atrium featuring a

The totem pole in the corporate lobby of LaSalle Plaza is by Native American artist George Morrison.

Four new towers sprang up, seemingly at once, to grace the Minneapolis skyline.

collage of City of Lakes images. A large stone staircase ascends to the skyway level, where a landing features a cone-shaped fountain of granite inlaid with copper and sandblasted Native American patterns. Of great appeal to members of the public entering from the LaSalle side is a massive totem by Native American artist George Morrison.

## The AT&T Tower

In July 1991 a shiny new green glass tower opened on Sixth and Marquette. The architects had splayed out each facet of the crown to give the tower animation to the sky. Viewers quickly dubbed it "the artichoke" or "the tulip" for its intricately designed crown.

Primarily built to house AT&T's then 1,000 Minnesota employees, the 34-story structure was designed by Walsh Bishop Associates, with Ryan Construction, Minneapolis, the developer. With two existing International Centre buildings down the block already connected to the Foshay Tower, the AT&T Tower became a new skyway link.

As for public space, Wayne Bishop explained that there was no room for a plaza outdoors, so the architects had planned major indoor public space at the corner atrium of the entry at Ninth and Marquette: "We raised the skirts of the building three stories up and provided an escalator for visitors to access the Leeann Chin restaurant on second. Then we designed six enormous columns of tinted green glass and illuminated them. The hexagonal columns, made of multifaceted green frosted glass, sat on a patterned Italian marble floor."

The design certainly created an elegant entrance for the tower, but it does not seem to be the kind of private/public space that invites the community in. After more than 20 years, the tower is still known as the AT&T.

## First Bank Place

The third of the early 1990s towers to rise was First Bank Place at 225 Sixth Street South. The tallest and biggest of the four, it opened with a flourish in early summer 1992. I was excited when I heard the name of the principal architect—James Freed of Pei Cobb Freed, who later designed the Holocaust Museum in Washington, D.C. The project (managing) architect was HKS Architects of Dallas.

The project was a challenge even for such renowned architects, as the tower had to combine three structures in one—a 56-story tower containing 31 floors for its major tenant, First Bank; an 18-story office building (The Park) for its major tenant and managing partner, IBM; and a 14-story atrium facing the Hennepin County Government Center, to link the two taller buildings.

The original public space in First Bank Place, now Capella Tower

All kinds of walkways, both private and public, weave through the complex, linking the tower to its neighbors. Directly opposite the Hennepin County Government Center Plaza is a major public space: a five-story atrium serving as a winter garden with benches, fountains, and a skyway level for shops.

According to James Freed, the design was nevertheless "really simple . . . using a connecting geometry of cylinders and cubes." In the design description, he wrote: "The three cylindrical components are centered on each of the quadrants of the L-shaped site. The geometry of the squares defines how sections are subtracted from the tower to create the profiles of First Bank Place."

The cubes are six-story grids of pinkish granite and silver, forming more traditional building blocks at the base. As the tower soars upward, the blocks are stripped back to reveal steel-and-glass cylinders of varying height. The tower tops off at 56 stories, one foot lower than the IDS and two-and-a-half-feet taller than César Pelli's Norwest Tower.

During the 1990s, it seemed, every new tower had to show a new and different top. Sure enough, Freed designed a metal-strutted circular crown as though signaling, "I'm a match for IDS or even better." At night, the crown gleams like a halo over downtown Minneapolis.

Since its debut, the skyscraper has been renamed twice. In 1997 it become US Bancorp Place, and in 2009 it became Capella Tower. Informally, people call it "the halo." The Star Tribune Media Company moved into three floors of the former IBM tower, henceforth to be known as the Star Tribune Building, where its headquarters overlook the Hennepin County Government Center and outdoor plaza.

## Dain Bosworth Plaza

The Dain Bosworth Plaza, built in 1992, contained office space and an upscale Neiman Marcus department store at its base. Shea Architects, Minneapolis, designed the store's four-level interior, making use of the finest materials available to express the elegance of Neiman Marcus. The firm certainly succeeded. I loved walking through Neiman's to admire the expensive fashion and the subtle simple design of this glamorous place.

Lohan Associates, Chicago, designed the 40-story tower to set back from the retail base and complement the Nicollet Mall with its modernist style. Built of sparkling green glass it is accented with silver spandrel glass panels at the top. Emphasizing the retail element is Indiana limestone, Cold Spring diamond pink granite outlining the windows, with a touch of white Vermont marble. Wine-colored awnings set off the street entrances.

"Our whole approach was to make the Nicollet Mall site a fun retail experience," said Brookfield Development of the project. On the second and fourth floors, the building provided connections to the skyway, other shops, and a restaurant.

In 2013 Neiman Marcus closed its store in Minneapolis. The tower gained new owners in 2014, to become the CenterPoint Energy Building; most of the CenterPoint employees will office there. The space once held for Neiman Marcus is to be the new home of tourist and convention bureau Meet Minneapolis and other tenants, however, the 40-story tower is now named RBC Tower.

This story draws from "Inner Space," published in my April 8, 1991, *Skyway News* column, *Changing Skyscapes.*

# 10 The Colonial Church of Edina 1996

I firmly believe that the spirits of the architects who pour talent and energy into their designs live on in the life of their buildings. Colonial Church of Edina, a national award-winning, postmodern expression of a New England village, is a prime example. This is where I go, years after my architect husband's death, to feel his contagiously witty spirit.

Richard Hammel, as principal architect, headed the HGA design team that made this unique church much more than a place for Christian worship. It is a community place for caring, learning, listening, and sharing.

In 1971, Dick Hammel and HGA design guru Ted Butler began studies for the original Colonial Church congregation, then mushrooming in growth as the result of the dynamic leadership of its minister, the Reverend Dr. Arthur A. Rouner Jr.

Many meetings later, in 1974, the congregation voted to buy a 23-acre site down the freeway from its original site. It still wanted a "puritan-style" building but also one with a variety of multipurpose spaces. That began the debate between Hammel and Rouner about the definition of "colonial" architecture. To resolve their differences, they traveled to Barnstable, Massachusetts, where Rouner, a native New Englander, knew of a church dating to the Pilgrims. Dick came home struck by the building's simplicity,

The national AIA award-winning Colonial Church of Edina won acclaim for Dick Hammel in *Time* magazine in 1980.

Exterior detail of the Colonial Church

determined to create a contemporary statement of Colonial Church's Puritan history.

HGA engineers began transforming the once swampy site into a private park. To bring the building to human-friendly scale, the design team grouped five gabled-roof components around an open courtyard. In the center, the team placed a freestanding bell tower as a symbolic element. The "village" housed a sanctuary or meetinghouse, seminar rooms, lounges, and a fellowship room, linked with a main street walkway. Warm, honey-colored woods were applied through the building. In the meetinghouse, the builders used exposed posts, beams, and trusses. The gray clapboard, white-trimmed church opened to wide acclaim in 1979.

In 1980, the AIA selected the church for national honors. The design attracted *Time* magazine in 1982 as an unusual work of religious architecture. When Dick was interviewed for the story, he said simply, "It is wonderful work because something other than dollars is valued. We are designing for the celebration of human life."

In the years following my husband's death, it seemed only natural. though I'm not a member, to drop into Colonial Church. One year I even joined the choir. But there in the choir loft I found it hard to sing for the lumps in my throat. While the music soared, I looked over the meetinghouse space, glowing with warmth and light, and felt Dick's presence around me.

This story draws from my article "Colonial Church of Edina" published in the 1996 AIA National Convention program. The convention met in the Twin Cities that year.

# 11 Abbey Church of Saint John the Baptist 1996

At first glimpse of the Abbey Church at Saint John's University, I am overwhelmed by the spiritual power of Marcel Breuer's architecture. The gigantic sculptural form in all its concrete simplicity speaks to the Benedictine belief in integrity, sanctity, and faith.

As Abbott Baldwin Dworschak said in 1953, "At its best, the Benedictine tradition challenges us to think boldly and to cast our ideals in forms [that] will be valid for generations to come."

Breuer, with his Bauhaus background and approach to modernism, readily won the commission in 1953 over other noted architects such as Walter Gropius and Eero Saarinen. According to my friend Brother Frank Kacmarcik, who assisted in the project, "Breuer didn't want an ordinary tower like the clichés of the past. He chose a slab, then turned the concrete slab on end, cantilevered it vertically on parabolic cross vaults, then inserted the bells."

Approaching the church, I see that the soaring bell tower stands in front, structurally separate, announcing the presence of God. The massive square parallelogram holding all that concrete weight appears to be graceful and light. Breuer said the concept became reality through the use of engineered concrete.

Breuer's stark simplicity imparts an atmosphere of serenity and peace to the interior.

Ascending several stone steps leading to a granite piazza, I stop below the bell banner to look over the countryside, wondering at this architecture that so invites me into its setting.

Entering the portal of the church, I step into a small space—a baptistery with recessed floor—again aware of the simplicity of Breuer's design: The concrete and granite walls, skylights, plants, running water, and a sculpture of Saint John. There is no other ornamentation. The light is subdued. Then, passing through massive wooden doors into the main church, I see the light and monumentality of a space unbroken by supporting columns.

The pews are built of three-inch-thick laminated oak. The altars are granite; the metalwork is bronze. What may at first seem stark becomes brilliance in the huge north honeybee wall, its stained-glass inserts cut and formed by local craftsmen. The black-robed monks quietly file into the church for prayer, completing the scene of serenity and peace. But the church, open to all faiths, can seat many more—nearly 2,000 during Sunday masses for students, monks, and visitors.

In the Abbey Church, architect Breuer, working with McGough Construction Company and members of the monastic community, created an expression of true modernism combined with monastic spirituality. There is no doubt the Abbey Church conveys the century-old tradition of the Benedictine community serving liturgical and community life.

Marcel Breuer, 1902–1981, was born in Hungary. He taught at the Bauhaus along with Ludwig Mies van der Rohe and Walter Gropius. Breuer left Germany in 1935 to join Gropius at Harvard University and later formed his own firm in New York, where he won a commission for the UNESCO Headquarters in Paris. Through his designs Breuer became noted for the use of honest materials, tubular steel, and bent plywood. In particular, he loved working with reinforced concrete.

According to curator Jennifer Olivares of the Minneapolis Institute of Arts, the Abbey Church is a "triumph of concrete engineering with its folded exterior walls."

Personally, I am always thrilled to visit this timeless landmark of modernism. Completed in 1961 at a time of transition for the Roman Catholic Church, its shape is like no other. Its simplicity evokes a feeling of spirituality, and I'm proud such a masterpiece evolved in Minnesota. When the monks raise their voices in song in this unique space, I realize why I make an annual pilgrimage to the Abbey Church at Saint John's University. In no way ordinary, it is a great cathedral in the heartland of America.

This story draws from my article "Abbey Church," published in *100 Places Plus 1: An Unofficial Architectural Survey of Favorite Minnesota Sites* (AIA Minnesota, 1996).

# 12 James J. Hill House
1996

From a bluff overlooking downtown Saint Paul, the sprawling James J. Hill House commands a splendid view of the Mississippi River and the transportation network that brought James J. Hill his fortune. Located near the Cathedral of Saint Paul at 240 Summit Avenue, the mansion seemed to me forbidding when my father took us on Sunday drives along Summit Avenue.

Perhaps that was because, in true Richardsonian Romanesque style, the exterior is of huge, variously sized blocks of Massachusetts red sandstone, creating a massive effect. Many years later, after visiting the sandstone house darkened over time, I completely changed my mind, realizing what the architects had accomplished in designing a family home for the famous "Empire Builder." It was also the largest home built on Summit Avenue, and it has remained so.

Casting aside the likes of local architects Cass Gilbert and Clarence Johnston, Hill chose a firm from Boston—Peabody, Stearns & Furber—challenging it to design interiors workable for his wife and ten children yet suitable for entertaining visiting notables. The powerful Hill was not a man to disagree with, and when the original architects overrode the plans of the stonecutters as to how the sandstone was to be cut and carved, he promptly fired them and hired another Boston firm—Irving

The "McMansion" of its time, Hill's huge home is Richardsonian Romanesque.

& Casson, charged mostly with the home's interior. The house was completed in 1891 with exceedingly tall chimneys, turrets, arches, gabled roofs, and an elegant porte cochere. The result is still impressive.

The main floor of the three-story house is especially engaging. I have always admired the art gallery, an elegant two-story space with a high ceiling. Using newly available technological advances, the builders installed a skylight complete with a retractable, canopied ceiling. A handsome pipe organ was built into the west end of the gallery. I have attended chamber music recitals in this room, marveling at its excellent acoustics.

Hill loved art and began collecting in the early 1880s, including many 19th-century French moderns such as Jean-Jacques Rousseau, Jean-François Millet, Gustave Courbet, and Eugène Delacroix. In addition, the works of Minnesota's notable artists, such as

Hill loved music and art. All those who visit the mansion will want to tour the well-lit art gallery, where a built-in pipe organ often is played.

Cameron Booth and Clara Mairs, grace these walls in changing exhibits of the Minnesota Historical Society's art collection.

Throughout the Hill House, ornate hand-carved woodwork is a distinguishing feature. Quartersawn white oak prevails—also mahogany—in the dining room, library, music room, and parlor. The floors are of thick maple. The fine craftsmanship of the place is obvious. Exquisitely carved mahogany decorates the entire formal dining room, where as many as 22 diners can sit under a gold-leafed ceiling surrounded by hand-tooled leather-covered walls. Chief woodcarver Johannes Kirchmayer gave his work a signature by carving his face into a front-door frame.

A 100-foot reception hall opens up from the entry to a grand staircase extending up two flights. The landing glows from six stained-glass windows fashioned in double-tiered panels.

Many functional features, considered marvels at the time, were built into the house. They include combination gas-and-electric lights, modern plumbing, central heating, 22 fireplaces (16 of them gas, the latest thing), and security systems. The total square footage of living space is 36,000, ample for a big family and equally large domestic staff.

After their parents' deaths in 1916 and 1921, four of Hill's daughters bought the house from the estate in 1925 and presented it to the Roman Catholic Archdiocese of Saint Paul and Minneapolis, which used it as an office, school, and residence. The house was named a National Historic Landmark in 1961. The Minnesota Historical Society (MHS) acquired the house from the archdiocese in 1978, began renovations continuing into the early 1980s, and opened it for tours. At last members of the general public could see this historic gem.

The MHS continues operation of the house, offering guided tours, concerts, and educational programs. A fine example of historic preservation, the James J. Hill House is a must for anyone interested in seeing how the family of one of Minnesota's pioneer business magnates—and its household help—lived.

This story draws from my article "James J. Hill House," published in *100 Places Plus 1: An Unofficial Architectural Survey of Favorite Minnesota Sites* (AIA Minnesota, 1996).

# 13 Winton Guest House 2010

Stepping into the Winton Guest House is like walking into art. Designed by Frank Gehry for D. Michael (Mike) and Penny Winton and completed in 1987, the little house is whimsical and practical at the same time. This delightful "folly" is composed of a series of diminutive spaces clustered under varied sculptural forms.

Entering through a red door for the first time, I saw the skylight in the pyramidal roof flooding the atrium with light. A wedge-shaped space contained a bedroom and bath, a curving "trapezoid" was an office or second bedroom, and a cube with a chimney comprising the cozy fireplace alcove. A spiral stairway adjoined a tiny kitchen leading to a sleeping loft.

When the Wintons asked Gehry to accept the commission for a small guesthouse, he consented, knowing it must complement their modern Lake Minnetonka home designed by Philip Johnson in 1953. The result was magic.

The exterior of the guesthouse of 1,800 square feet stirs the imagination though its materials are simple: Brick clads the fireplace area and chimney (echoing the brick of the main house). Plywood covers the office. Metal shielding protects the truncated pyramid roof. Next to the welcoming entry, the kitchen and

Guests enter the little house via a door leading directly into the atrium. An eggplant-colored FinnPly garage sits neatly alongside.

rectangular garage are covered with FinnPly. The guesthouse was completed in 1987.

Standing in the office of the guesthouse, looking out at the lake, I exclaimed to a visitor, "It's so much fun to be inside this house." We agreed that guests would love to live there for an extended stay.

After many years of enjoying both houses, the Wintons decided to move back to Minneapolis. New owner/developer Kurt Woodhouse subdivided the property, separating the guesthouse from the main house. For some time the guesthouse sat empty, but Woodhouse was determined to save it. Ultimately, he felt that members of the public should be able to see the unique structure: "Art of this caliber is meant to be enjoyed by the public and to inspire a greater appreciation of modern art in many forms."

In 2008, Woodhouse gave the guesthouse to the University

of Saint Thomas at the Daniel C. Gainey Conference Center in Owatonna, Minnesota. Moving the building some 80 miles was complex and costly and wasn't accomplished until 2010. Stubbs Building Movers cut the house into eight pieces at a reported cost of $1 million. Reassembling it was also difficult.

Architect Gehry seemed satisfied when he saw the house in its new setting—on flat land surrounded by fields of grass and groups of trees. I greeted him there, asking whether the site was okay. He replied that he was glad people would be able to tour the guesthouse.

In August 2014, the University of Saint Thomas sold the Owatonna property minus the guesthouse, with an agreement to relocate it within two years. Faced with a dilemma and no room on its campuses, the university announced in February 2015 that the guesthouse was to be dismantled again and sold at auction for up to $1.5 million plus moving costs. It sold to an unknown bidder from outside Minnesota for $905,000, including auction fees but not moving costs.

This story draws from my chapter on the guesthouse in *Legendary Homes of Lake Minnetonka* (Minnesota Historical Society Press, 2010).

# 14 Davis/Winton/Nelson House 2010

While selecting homes to portray in *Legendary Homes of Lake Minnetonka*, I spotted from my boat a true modern classic. High on a meadow-covered hillside sat a low rectangular brick home with flat roof, broad windows, and absolutely no ornamentation. Sure enough, Philip Johnson, early champion of the international style and designer of the IDS Tower, was its architect. Richard Davis, curator of the Minneapolis Institute of Arts, wanted a home of that style to house his art collection and convinced Johnson to design it for him in 1953.

After contacting the current owners, I was invited see their home, which was every bit as elegant in its simplicity as I thought it would be.

In 2002, Bob and Carolyn Nelson bought the 11-acre property from Mike and Penny Winton, who had enjoyed the house for 36 years. The Nelsons, former Minnesotans who met at Carleton College, were looking for a modernist house suitable for displaying their pre-Columbian art collection. Bob Nelson, newly retired from GE's management team in Connecticut, was convinced that the house was structurally sound. They loved the ceilings and floors of terrazzo and teak; all they needed to do was refurbish the kitchen and add new shelving and bookcases.

Gehry's design for the guesthouse complements Philip Johnson's 1950s modern design for the Davis House.

The couple greeted me cordially in the teak-lined entry and led me into the "great room." I immediately noticed the sweeping walls of glass that let in the sun to light the interior. The Nelsons also appreciated Johnson's original plan for two distinctive wings: The main section is a spacious rectangle containing living and dining areas, master suite, and two other bedrooms. In the center is the highlight of the space—an indoor atrium that Johnson had designed for his first-ever house in a northern clime. With glass walls and ceiling, the atrium is a winter garden covered by a gridded translucent canopy. The smaller wing houses the kitchen, two smaller bedrooms, and the passageway to a garage.

Flanking the L-shaped interior is an elegant square patio with a long, narrow pool and one beautiful birch tree overlooking Lake Minnetonka.

The Nelsons needed a certain amount of remodeling for the

Philip Johnson designed this sunny indoor atrium for what he called his first "winter house."

house to fit their lifestyle. To manage the project, the new owners hired Suzanne Ritus, a Miami-based industrial designer. She loved the linear quality of the house and the way the architect opened vistas to the lake while providing maximum wall space for art. Her work involved installing new bookcases, shelving for art, designing a small entertainment center, converting two bedrooms into offices for Bob and Carolyn, and updating the powder room. The project also involved completely redoing the kitchen; now it is a shiny GE Monogram kitchen, appropriate given Bob's earlier career with the company. Ritus tore out the original Congoleum floor and replaced it with travertine and installed air-conditioning, completing the project in less than eight months.

Midcentury modern furnishings chosen for the house include a Mies van der Rohe black leather couch, two Barcelona chairs in beige, and eight Brno black-leather dining chairs lining the long Italian-made oak dining table.

Thirteen years later, the Nelsons can enjoy their house summer and winter. They are glad they kept the house true to its original design yet modified it to suit their specific tastes. The character of the house enhances its natural site.

This story draws from my chapter on the Davis/Nelson/Winton house published in *Legendary Homes of Lake Minnetonka* (Minnesota Historical Society Press, 2010).

# 15 Minneapolis Federal Building and U.S. Courthouse 1997

One ambitious 1990s building in downtown Minneapolis is the Federal Building and U.S. Courthouse by Bill Pedersen, Minnesota native and founding partner of KPF, New York. The building is set in a historic district including the landmark Flour Exchange Building.

I like the way the architect set the courthouse well back from its neighbor across the street—the Richardsonian Romanesque Municipal Building (Minneapolis City Hall and Hennepin County Courthouse) as if in recognition of its similar functions. Occupying most of a city block, the modern courthouse serves in pleasing contrast, yet conveys strength, simplicity, and respect for the judiciary.

National security codes, established after the 1995 Oklahoma City bombing, disallowed wide-open plazas in front of federal buildings. So rather than a traditional courthouse with columns and pediments, it is a modern interpretation of civic classicism.

The General Service Administration (GSA) requested that the plaza evoke Minnesota's natural history. Clad in limestone-like precast concrete, low-E insulated glass, and anodized aluminum, the block-long tower and its sizable plaza make a powerful

Minneapolis Federal Building and U. S. Courthouse, 1997:
The new courthouse, designed by KPF, New York, brought
modern classicism to the city's most historic district.

statement. According to Pedersen, the overall mass of the building pulls away from City Hall as much as possible to form a generous landscaped public plaza in counterpoint to the new facility.

In back, the structure curves out over Third Street to accommodate federal judges on the upper floors (according to the required allocation) and district judges below. There are two courtrooms per floor, public courtroom galleries, separate central prisoner elevators, and holding cells and offices on lower floors. On a tour of the building, I admired the elegance of the courtroom areas, finished in cherry-veneer paneling and millwork, muted carpeting, acoustic wall and ceiling treatment, and direct/indirect lighting. On that day, both Judge Diane Murphy and Judge James Rosenbaum spoke highly of their handsome new offices.

Administrative offices are housed in a blocklike form at the tower's base along with a cafeteria on Third Avenue. Security, support, holding cells, and related functions are located below grade.

## The Courthouse Plaza

At first, the landscaped courthouse plaza drew a lot of laughs and some caustic remarks regarding its "Indian mounds." Landscape architect Martha Schwartz of Massachusetts indignantly explained that the mounds recall part of Minnesota's landscape known as glacial drumlins. Those who recognize Schwartz as an artist who uses landscape as her media were not surprised by the controversy. They find the plaza bold and fun, engaging and lively. Others do not.

The designer, who did research with Native American tribes in the state, planted the tear-shaped earth mounds with small jack pine trees and narcissus, suggesting a field of glacial drumlims. Alongside the mounds are log benches stained silver to represent

Artist Tom Otterness created several whimsical sculptures scattered over the plaza to add interest to the landscaped drumlins.

the state's lumber-industry heritage. Black-and-buff-striped concrete pavers guide visitors into the courthouse. Figuring out how to keep plants on the roof of a parking garage must have been quite a challenge. This was Schwartz's solution.

Judge Rosenbaum (now retired), who took daily walks around town, commented that he often saw people enjoying their lunches on the plaza. He was pleased to see how children loved to play there and especially to make faces at the small works of art scattered among the earthworks. The whimsical sculptures represent real-life situations as presented by artist Tom Otterness. Several years after the plaza's debut, the GSA added comfortable, gray metallic outdoor benches to the area.

Countering the views of those amused by the mounds is that by award-winning Minneapolis architect Milo Thompson: "People may think it's a bit bizarre, but once they learn what was intended, I think they'll find it extremely engaging."

The Federal Building and U.S. Courthouse won a 1996 design award from the GSA, as did the plaza. But from my point of view, the drumlins do resemble mounds.

This story draws from my article "Martha Schwartz Designs New U.S. Courthouse Plaza in Minneapolis," published in the April 1997 issue of *Architectural Record.*

# 16 Heinävaara Finnish Elementary 1999

Not often does an architectural firm design a building I would describe as charming. But I find one of that description in my list of 1999 stories. It is an elementary school designed by Cuningham Group—not in Minnesota but in Heinävaara, Finland, a town along the Russian border depending for its growth on the forests of North Karelia.

How did John Cuningham's Minneapolis firm land this completely unexpected commission? The answer is in my story in the September 1999 issue of *Architectural Record;*

## The Heinävaara School

In 1997 Bruce Jilk, then an educational facilities specialist at Cuningham Group, was invited to make a presentation in Helsinki about the pressing need for schools to change internally and externally in support of better learning. A Finnish architect and the mayor of Heinävaara listened intently to his theories embodying the latest architectural techniques and construction methods. They were already planning a new elementary school for their district, one with the customary Finnish double-loaded corridors and closed-in classrooms.

Heinävaara Finnish Elementary, 1999:
The completed school extends over the landscape
with learning studios, each with a gabled roof,
supporting the students desire for a school
that feels like home.

Mayor Juhani Rouvinen and architect Antero Turkki decided to visit a U.S. firm that was building wood schools with the new techniques. After some research, they chose Cuningham Group. When they arrived, Judith Hoskens, a Cuningham Group school specialist and the mother of two young children, met with the two Finns.

"We hit it off," said Hoskens, who realized they wanted not only a modern school but also one built entirely of wood, so as to boost the local forest industry.

After making a proposal for a new school with open-learning classrooms and flexible spaces of varying size, Cuningham's firm gained the commission. Soon Hoskens took off for Finland as project architect.

The mayor called a halt to the traditional design, telling 150 people at a town meeting, "We need to get this job done right from the beginning." He stressed that they must use the American technique of platform framing rather than the traditional balloon-framed construction.

Judy Hoskens was pleased that the community was involved. At first there were objections to the new plan, but the Minnesota architects helped to create a shared vision. It was a radical change for the Finns, who were used to seeing their children sit in rows in closed classrooms.

For Hoskens, it was a meaningful design challenge. She and her team devised "learning studios" that open to a bright, airy, central gathering space running the length of the school. That became the media center/performance space and cafeteria. Other learning spaces supported hands-on individual and group learning. A stage opened to the gym and cafeteria, adaptable for the community. Computers on mobile tables could be wheeled around to support learning anywhere, anytime. Clerestory windows brightened the space in this school located at a latitude of limited winter light.

A unique feature near the school's entrance—a 10-foot-high Karelian oven/fireplace that can be used by students to bake traditional pies—is also the biggest hit with the community. The mayor's son, who attended the school, told his father the new school felt so much like home he had a hard time leaving at the end of the day.

Cuningham Group sent along a group of six contractors to help build the all-wood school. With platform framing, in which the first story built provides a platform for the rest, construction is faster and more economical than with balloon-style construction.

The schools' exterior is pine, with a delightful, ornate wooden canopy, reminiscent of the Russian Orthodox architecture of the region, painted bright red, and providing shelter for students and teachers who often cross-country ski to school. Inside, each learning studio, with gabled roof, supports the desire of the students for a school that feels like home in both scale and form.

The 26,000-square-foot finished school, opened in 1998 to house 160 students, is undoubtedly the smallest of all Cuningham's education projects, but as Judy Hoskens says, "This was a rare gem of a commission."

John Cuningham proudly notes, "We designed it, and we built it."

This story draws from my article "Cuningham Crosses Cultures to Build a School in Finland," in the news section of the September 1999 issue of *Architectural Record*.

# 17 Renaissance on the River
2001

While I was reporting for *Skyway News* in the early 1990s, I learned that Saint Paul's leaders were alarmed that the city might be losing out to the suburbs. It was time for a visionary plan—one that would bring the city back to its biggest asset, the Mississippi River. I wrote about that vision in the September 2001 issue of *Architectural Record:*

## A Renaissance on the River in Saint Paul

Minnesota's capital city, Saint Paul, is in the midst of a renaissance, thanks to the masterful plan *Saint Paul on the Mississippi Development Framework.* With the plan as basis, once-forlorn areas along Saint Paul's 27-mile-riverfront are being rejuvenated. The plan touts far-reaching goals, spelling out ways in which to revive the downtown core and re-evoke the city's image as a thriving river town. Results are now evident. How did the plan succeed?

Founded on limestone bluffs overlooking the Mississippi in 1851, Saint Paul thrived for many years. People flocked to the river for steamboat rides, picnics on Harriet Island, fishing and boating.

Minnesota's most renowned architect, Cass Gilbert, in designing the Minnesota State Capitol at the beginning of the 20th century, visualized a crescent-shaped network of tree-lined avenues

The first completed project of the renaissance was a new Wabasha Street Bridge, constructed in 1998 to connect the city with Harriet Island Regional Park and beyond.

radiating from the capitol to the river. As the city grew, however, buildings fronted away from the river and industrial pollution contaminated it.

By the mid-1990s, action was needed, and certain dedicated business and community leaders, under the leadership of Mayor Norm Coleman, made a major decision in hiring planner Ken Greenberg, of Urban Strategies, Toronto.

When Greenberg first saw the city in 1994, he felt "a sense of disinvestment, the loss of jobs and population, and a downtown seriously hollowed out." He forged a team of 30-plus organizations already involved, key members from city planning and parks and public works, Capitol City Partnership, the Saint Paul Port Authority, and the newly formed Saint Paul Riverfront Corporation (SPRC). To guide design principles, the city and SPRC established the Saint Paul Design Center.

The plan, *Saint Paul on the Mississippi Development Framework,* coordinated by the SPRC and the design center and released in 1997, spelled out "a system of interconnected mixed-use urban villages nestled in the lush green of a reforested river valley." Based on principles of city building such as evoking a sense of place, restoring the urban ecology, and investing in the public realm, the plan targeted specific areas for development. The total cost for what later was named the Renaissance Project was just over $190 million, raised by private/public investment, for more than three dozen components to be built in stages over five to ten years.

The first completed project was a new Wabasha Street Bridge, renamed the Wabasha Street Freedom Bridge in 2002. Designed by Saint Paul Public Works and TKDA Architects and built in 1998, the wide, sweeping bridge featured extra-wide sidewalks and overlook plazas. Greenberg called the bridge "a great city balcony, a key turning point in the way the city thinks of itself."

Almost everyone liked the red-painted bridge. My family and I had waited a year for its completion; on opening day my daughter, Susan, her infant daughter, Caleigh, and I plus many excited Saint Paulites, walked across the span and back.

As a catalyst for development, the rebuilt bridge brought about the rebirth of Harriet Island, originally the city's great gathering place. Although the park's amenities had fallen into neglect over the years, the river had been greatly cleaned up thanks to decade-long storm-water management, flood control, and other programs. One outstanding improvement was the restoration of the 1941 pavilion designed by Minnesota's first African-American architect (and the country's first African-American municipal architect), Clarence Wigington, and renamed in his honor. The shoreline was redesigned with a terraced plaza leading down to the river. Crowds attended the opening of the refurbished 70-acre park. In 2000 it was renamed Harriet Island Regional Park.

A new band shell was funded for the island, and a big name in architecture—AIA Gold Medalist Michael Graves—designed it. The Target Stage is an open-air stage for the performing arts placed in an accessible corner of the park. Inspired by the lattice steel-frame bridges that once spanned the river and the Saint Paul Cathedral dome, Graves, in association with Rafferty, Rafferty & Tollefson (now RRTL Architects), Saint Paul, devised a bold scheme: two red web-steel-framed towers supporting a suspended roof of copper..

On the adjacent Raspberry Island where the Schubert Club, Saint Paul Chamber Orchestra, and others were scheduled to perform, noted glass artist James Carpenter, New York, designed a striking glass arch structure that curved around the site, appropriately named the Schubert Club Band Shell.

A crucial part of the main plan was construction of the near $100 million Science Museum of Minnesota, designed by

Ellerbe Becket. When completed late in 1999, it was the first public structure in Saint Paul with direct access to the river. The seven-story brick, stone, and glass building meets the riverfront through a series of indoor and outdoor stairways and terraces. At street level, a brick façade encases a convertible-dome Omnitheatre. The science museum, noted for its spectacular exhibitions, remains one of the state's most popular cultural attractions.

Although the committee called Greenberg "our great facilitator," he directly attributed the plan's success to the framework team. Patrick Seeb, executive director of the Saint Paul Riverfront Corporation, said the results of plan were due to the "vision, leadership, stewardship, and the input of thousands of citizens." More than 3,000 units of new housing were built in accordance with the framework.

"We identified the crescent of opportunity in Cass Gilbert's grand axis extending from the capitol to the river," said Greenberg. While some called it "Cass Gilbert Revisited," the master planner from Urban Strategies emphasized, "Thanks to the work of a lot of people, this city is transforming itself."

This story draws from my article "A Renaissance on the River in Saint Paul," published in the September 2001 issue of *Architectural Record.*

# 18 Science Museum of Minnesota 1999

The first building to take advantage of the Saint Paul riverfront was the Science Museum of Minnesota, one of the region's most respected cultural institutions. Opening in 1999 after five years in the planning, the building perches smack on a bluff of the Mississippi River, where it commands sweeping views of the Mississippi River valley.

The massive, seven-story, brick, stone, and glass structure of block-shaped forms cascades to the river in dramatic fashion, accented with outdoor terraces and elevators, indoors and out.

David Loehr, then principal architect for Ellerbe Becket's design team, said, "We organized this building with two faces: the city face and the river face." For the river side, the architects carefully chose stone that echoes the warm colors of the bluff. On the Kellogg Boulevard side, they created a civic presence with a large landscaped plaza and a huge glass façade looking towards Rice Park. Although it is not the icon that some museums have become today, it is a strong statement inviting the public to see what science is all about.

Thanks to the public/private funding of the $100 million project by state, city, corporate, individuals, and foundations, the museum has several public amenities. One is a monumental 120-step grand stairway for pedestrian access all the way down to the

Science
Museum

The plan's major accomplishment was building the $100,000,000 Science Museum of Minnesota in 1999. It was the first civic structure leading directly down to the river.

river. Since its opening, I have visited this popular museum many times, noticing that few of the crowds of visitors walk down all the steps, but it's worth a try. Another outdoor amenity is a landscaped science park at the lower street level, complete with minigolf, another opportunity for learning.

Inside, many banks of elevators carry visitors from floor to floor in the complex. With classrooms, a youth science center, labs, a 330-seat auditorium, and general meeting/eating area at its entrance, the second level of the museum is entirely devoted to schoolchildren. School buses, more then 140 a day, enter a circular entrance at the Chestnut Street entrance to drop off their young charges.

It's always fun to visit the science museum, especially with children. My grandson, Danny, loved the dinosaurs as well as the hands-on weather tools that let him use fog and a stream of water to see how clouds are formed.

The architects purposely designed the museum in an open-warehouse style so visitors can easily choose which galleries they want to visit. The same openness gives museum staff members the flexibility they need in accommodating specific exhibits—hanging dinosaurs, devices that youngsters can twist and turn, and so forth.

The human health gallery, featuring tissues, organs, and systems in the body, is of particular interest to me. Another I like, especially when I'm with my grandchildren, is the River Gallery, designed to educate us about river ecology and geography. For young children, the big attraction is the authentic 1944 Mississippi River towboat, perched on a 75-foot high balcony just outside the gallery. Youngsters love climbing aboard the tugboat and pretending to steer it. From that vantage, you can look down two levels to the Great Hall, a glass-enclosed atrium where the dinosaurs hold court.

As the most popular museum in Minnesota, the Science Museum, designed in an open warehouse style by Ellerbe Becket, attracts young and old to its many diverse galleries.

The big brick-clad boxlike structure to the right (west) of the Kellogg Boulevard entrance contains the museum's Omnitheatre, one of the first convertible-dome omnitheaters in the country. Ellerbe Becket engineers devised an ingenious structure that quickly converts the domed screen to a flat Imax screen. Seating accommodates 440.

During my first tour of the museum, which opened in 1999, I was told in an ironic note that Tom Ellerbe, pioneer leader of the architectural firm bearing his name, chose this very site on Kellogg Boulevard in 1931 for a proposed science museum "with no windows to block out the squalor below." I commend Ellerbe for his early vision. Wouldn't he be thrilled with what the Ellerbe architects of the late 1990s have accomplished here with the high-performance glass revealing the great vistas below! The glass allows only 28 percent of the sunlight and heat to reach the inside.

Today the Science Museum of Minnesota, with its many thought-provoking and interactive exhibits, literally packs them in. During the year 2014, the museum saw more than a million visitors. It is a key element of the city's renaissance.

This story draws from my article "Science in the Year 2000" in my November 24, 1999, *Skyway News* column, *Changing Skyscapes.*

# 19 Maya Lin's Minneapolis Roomscape 2003

Maya Lin, designer of the Vietnam Memorial in Washington

Minneapolis likes, on occasion, to show off its vaunted arts and culture, so it was no surprise when the city decided to label Third Avenue the "Avenue of the Arts." In 2001, the city called on property owners to use their buildings' façades to display works of art.

One major sponsor, American Express Financial (AEF) Corporation (now Ameriprise), agreed this was a great idea and decided to incorporate art into its new building on the corner of Tenth Street and Third Avenue South. Not only that—a member of the firm's advisory committee decided it was time to think big. Why not retain Maya Lin—the artist and architect who at age 21 created the Vietnam Veterans Memorial in Washington D.C., in 1982—for the work? After meeting with Lin, the advisors were convinced of her singular ability to combine art and architecture. The company announced her commission in 2001.

Lin was to design a winter garden, an indoor glassed-in landscape—*the character of a hill, under glass*—for all to see, in one corner of the AEF's new Client Services Building. Twenty years after her triumph in D.C. and with many award-winning commissions to her credit, Lin was ready for another project involving architecture.

When I first heard of the commission, I contacted *Architectural Record* to suggest a story about the commission. The news editor was noncommittal, but he gave me Maya Lin's contact number, and she agreed to an interview.

I arrived at her studio several stories up in an old stone building in the SoHo area of Manhattan, feeling nervous about meeting this brilliant young architect. I found Lin bent over her work in the middle of a serene open space. She greeted me quietly and motioned to her little girl to stay in the other room. I immediately relaxed. It struck me that she was just like the typical working mother, busy with work and worrying about day care for her daughter and how things were going at home (somewhere else in the city).

Soon Lin focused on the Minneapolis project. Bending over the table, she showed me her models for the proposed installation. Water, hills, and glass were its major elements. What did she mean by *the character of a hill, under glass*? She explained that a childhood spent in the gently rolling hills of Ohio inspired her work with landscape. She was striving "to slightly alter one's perception of the landscape."

"The client asked me to create an inside refuge for people to get away from their work, a place that brings the outside in," she said. After her intense description of the model for this contemplative work, I left her studio feeling I couldn't wait to see the final expression.

Months later, in Minneapolis, Lin finished the work. AEF planned a special art opening in 2002 and announced that the artist would be present. "Come see our winter garden," the invitation read. The advisors wanted a place of serenity within

A unique feature of Lin's design is the floor of laminated maple undulating like a gentle rolling hillside.

the hectic business building, said Barry Murphy, executive vice president of AEF Advisors.

For the floor's design, Lin asked herself, "What happens when you take a gentle rolling hillscape and bring it inside?" The result was a laminated maple floor undulating like gentle waves on the sea. She "planted" black olive trees on the hills and a few granite benches alongside them. The sculptural landscape, 28 by 55 feet, is of narrow maple floorboards laid over an egg-carton grid of thinly laid plywood.

The next major part of the installation is the water wall. I think this is what intrigues viewers who see the water flowing down the glass as they walk by. In summer, when a ribbon of water streams down the inside of the glass wall into an L-shaped pool, they enjoy the refreshing sound of falling water. In winter, when the water flowing over the exterior freezes, they enjoy the continually changing ice patterns on the sparkling glass. The concept of

When Maya Lin was commissioned by AEF to create a winter garden, *the character of a hill, under glass*, she installed a unique feature—water flowing both inside and outside the space.

the water wall was innovative to Minneapolis viewers but not to Lin, who has featured water in many of her works. One example is the *Women's Table* at Yale University in 1993, where water flows over sculptures and visitors are encouraged to touch and make ripples on the surface.

While AEF was originally developing plans for its new client services 14-story tower—designed by HKS Architects of Dallas with RSP Architects of Minneapolis for the interior—the company included a three-story public space shaped like a cube off the entry lobby. Visitors would have easy access to the art at the corner of Third Avenue and Tenth Street South. When Lin first became involved with the project, however, she decided the cube must be modified in proportion for the structural framing and glass curtain wall to provide a lighter, more ethereal effect.

RSP took it from there, working out the technical detailing to meet Lin's requirements. Engineers explained that while water walls were common, no one had ever tried freezing water on exterior glass. Lin persisted in learning about Minnesota's icy winters and selected her own consultants. Contractors then built the curtain wall to withstand a quarter inch of ice on the exterior glass. When the water occasionally freezes, the water wall develops icicles on its surface.

Outside on the Tenth Street corner is a small outdoor landscape designed by Lin's team—RSP and Damon Farber Associates of Minneapolis. Planted with grass and river birch, the landscape features a path of flamed granite leading to the entrance of the winter garden. Water from the curtain wall spills into a small pool bubbling at the street's edge.

Today Ameriprise limits public access to the winter garden to clients and invited groups, but employees still enjoy the space for relaxation and visual inspiration during normal company hours. Lin says she hopes guests will step out on the wavy floor to feel what it's like to walk over the hilly landscape usually found only outdoors.

"All I'm after," she says, "is to make people rethink what is reality."

---

This story draws from my article "Groundswells and Water Walls," published in the September/October 2003 issue of *Architecture Minnesota.*

# Part III: Encounters and Travels

# 20 Starchitects

Over the years I have gone to several AIA national conventions at which I was able to attend press conferences and other events held for accomplished architects, among them Frank Gehry, Lord Norman Foster, I. M. Pei, and César Pelli. At sundry other events, I heard lectures by Michael Graves, Jean Nouvel and Bill Pedersen. To these "starchitects," I add a Dick Hammel pick—David Salmela, one of Minnesota's own.

## Frank Gehry

Of the many starchitects I've met, my favorite is Frank Gehry. Despite his worldwide fame, he is low-key, casual, friendly, and loves to be with artists and people who are passionate about art and architecture. Thanks to Lyndel King's influence as director and chief curator of the Frederick R. Weisman Art Museum at the University of Minnesota, the Twin Cities community claims the first art museum designed by Gehry in the United States.

The Weisman's building site must have inspired him. Perched on a bluff overlooking the Mississippi River, the stainless-steel building completed in 1993 of curving and irregular shape stands as a new art form. Students laughingly call it the "Tin Man," though its back is clad in red brick to merge with the mainly brick buildings of the university campus.

Frank Gehry

The Weisman is where I have met and talked with Frank Gehry. On one unforgettable occasion, I had just returned from a tour of Spain and Portugal, where I inadvertently heard our Lisbon guide say, "We are going to have a new theater built here by a famous American architect, Mr. Frank Gehry."

Back home, I couldn't resist approaching Gehry and mentioning the Lisbon theater rumor. He stopped dead and said, "How did you ever get that information?"

I told him about the guide. He smiled and replied, "Well, that project just fell through." Later I was able to compliment him on the power and magic of his Bilbao museum.

Minnesotans have another connection with Frank Gehry in the imaginative guesthouse he designed for the Winton family at Lake Minnetonka in 1987. According to James Dayton, who earlier worked for Gehry's firm on the Disney Concert Hall, "The Winton Guest House is one of the three best buildings in Minnesota and of the 20th century."

## Lord Norman Foster

Norman Foster struck me as the perfect English gentleman. He treated all of us as media equals, politely answering questions despite my lowly freelance status. AIA president L. William Chapin II described Foster as a uniquely modern architect, one who found elegance in high technology and applied it to skyscrapers, art galleries, airports, and office buildings.

Foster remarked at one press conference: "Architecture has the

Lord Norman Foster

power to enhance the lives of the people it touches." He stressed the importance of collaboration with others—architects, engineers, clients, and contractors—and noted how vital it is to use light in a controlled way.

Having visited the massive airport he designed in Shanghai, I realize just how brilliant he is.

## I. M. Pei

I've always been awestruck by I. M. Pei's beautiful modernist design of the east wing of the National Gallery of Art in Washington, D.C. *New York Times* critic Ada Louise Huxtable called it "a palatial statement of the creative accommodation of contemporary art and architecture."

Because Pei was widely known as the master of modern architecture, I was fascinated by his speech describing his work and the importance of the art of architecture at the 1983 AIA National Convention in New York. Among his other well-known designs are the Kennedy Library in Boston and the glass-and-steel pyramid for the Louvre, in Paris. His firm, Pei Cobb Freed & Partners, has become one of the most distinguished architectural firms in America.

I. M. Pei

## Michael Graves

Michael Graves, once called the rock star of architecture, is noted for creating the first postmodern building in the United States. Minnesotans, especially, became aware of his designs for kitchen tools—his iconic teakettle, playful ice bucket, and other items sold at Target. In 2006, working with RSP Architects of Minneapolis, Graves designed another addition to the Minneapolis Institute of Arts—the new postmodern Target Wing.

Michael Graves

When I went to hear Graves speak in Minneapolis that year, I was shocked to see him sitting in a wheelchair, but he was still talking about the necessity for architects to design beautiful furniture—now for hospital rooms that are easy and comfortable for patients and caregivers. Later I learned he was struck in 2003 with a virus that caused paralysis from the waist down. Michael Graves died on March 12, 2015. He was an architect for whose work all of America's seniors can be grateful.

## César Pelli

Pelli is undoubtedly the most charming architect on my list. I well remember meeting the handsome Argentinian in San Francisco, when my husband, Dick Hammel, became a fellow of the AIA. Years later, in 1985, César Pelli won a coveted Minneapolis commission to design a bank building for the site where the 1929 Northwestern National Bank had burned on Thanksgiving Day 1982.

Open-air interior of Bruce Abrahamson's cedar-clad cabin

Lighting installed beneath the Stone Arch Bridge highlights the builder's achievement and adds drama to the city's waterfront.

Ordway Center for the Performing Arts

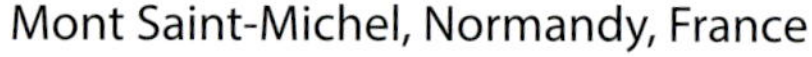

Mont Saint-Michel, Normandy, France

Château de Chambord, Loire Valley, France

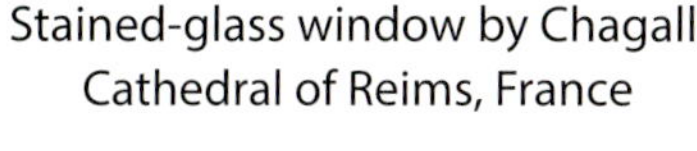

Stained-glass window by Chagall,
Cathedral of Reims, France

Dain Bosworth Plaza
(now RBC Plaza), 40 stories,
Lohan Associates, Minneapolis

AT&T Tower, 34 stories,
Walsh Bishop Associates, Minneapolis

First Bank Place (now Capella Tower), also provided quarters for IBM, 53 stories, Pei Cobb Freed & Partners, Minneapolis.

LaSalle Plaza, 30 stories, Ellerbe Becket (now AECOM), Minneapolis

Colonial Church of Edina, national award-winner for Richard Hammel

The interior design of the church reflects colonial influences in the way the central space, filled with light, surrounds the sanctuary with seating and an expanded choir loft from which singers fill the room with music.

Abbey Church of Saint John the Baptist, Marcel Breuer, Collegeville, Minnesota

Stained glass, cut and formed by local craftsmen, was inserted into a honeycomb wall to bring brilliant light to what might otherwise be a stark entrance.

Close-up of the Winton Guest House, a winsome sculpture

Classic 1950s furniture such as a Mies van der Rohe sofa is featured in the Nelsons' Johnson-designed house.

Amusing sculptures and glacial drumlins create interest on the huge plaza of the Minneapolis Federal Building and U.S. Courthouse.

This charming elementary school in Heinävaara, Finland, was designed and built by the Cuningham Group, Minneapolis.

The popular Science Museum of Minnesota, by Ellerbe Becket, opened in 1999.

The Frederick R. Weisman Art Museum was completed in 1993. Architect Frank Gehry playfully curved its stainless steel façade along the river for his first museum in the United States.

Maya Lin, known for her creation of the Vietnam Veterans Memorial in Washington, D.C., designed an indoor glass-room landscape for AEF (now Ameriprise) on Third Avenue, Minneapolis.

French architect Jean Nouvel, working with the Architectural Alliance, Minneapolis, designed the dramatic new Guthrie Theater, completed in 2006.

The Treasury at Petra, is one of the astonishing buildings carved from the red rock of this ancient city in Jordan.

The great columns of Karnak, Luxor, Egypt, fascinate architects from all over the world.

Bill Pedersen's design of the tower at 333 West Wacker Drive, with its breathtaking curve along the Chicago River, helped establish him as a champion skyscraper architect.

Native-created totem poles are preserved in Vancouver's Museum of Anthropology, designed by 1960s modernist Arthur Erickson. This is one of several poles in Stanley Park.

Dubrovnik was bombed heavily during the Bosnia War. Its tiled roofs sustained great damage.

A close-up of the tiles after renewal reveals the expertise of the Dubrovnik restoration.

Dubrovnik, "The Pearl of the Adriatic," stands out for the red-tiled roofs blanketing the city.

Hagia Sophia, with its massive dome, marks the entrance to Istanbul. For a thousand years a Byzantine church, then a mosque, and now a museum, the "Church of Holy Wisdom" is the city's top tourist attraction.

Under the massive dome, a brilliant design of mosaic tiles glimmers across the ceiling, adding to the wealth of Byzantine decoration displayed in this huge edifice.

Calatrava, who is known for his skeleton-inspired elements, designed the City of Arts and Sciences in Valencia, Spain, using crisscrossing white steel rods to create an airy, light-infusing effect.

Viewing Saint Paul from the High Bridge near my childhood home in Cherokee Park, I am reminded of all that this historic river town has meant to me. It's not just the lure of the Mississippi River or the Minnesota State Capitol. It has always been my hometown.

Calatrava's impressive work in Valencia—the City of Arts and Sciences—sparks amazement for its futuristic design. The dome—*L'Hemisferic*—is a planetarium with aluminum panels that open and close like an eyelid.

César Pelli

Pelli's new tower rose 50 stories in dramatic 1980s modern style with a touch of 1930s art deco. Everyone was well pleased by, even thrilled with, the result. Pelli gave Minneapolis an elegant sculpted skyscraper, slim and tall, of Minnesota Kasota stone with accents of white marble. Best of all, it was dramatically lit across wide portions of the top. Now known as the Wells Fargo Center, the tower was completed in 1989.

Pelli soon won another prized Minneapolis competition, for the design of a new Minneapolis Central Library (now Hennepin County Central Library), between Hennepin and Nicollet Avenues. Previous to his selection, the Minneapolis Library Board heard from seven architecture firms and their teams.

As a freelance reporter, I attended all the presentations. The competitors were local firms teamed with national firms. All were compelling. But Architectural Alliance had partnered with Pelli, and when he began describing his vision for a library complete with soaring glass atrium, airplane roof extending over the street, and glass elevators, I knew he and the Alliance had won. The library board was entranced as much by Pelli's charm as by the scheme he and his partners had conceived. The new library opened to the public in 2006.

## Jean Nouvel

French architect Jean Nouvel was new to Minnesota's architectural scene at the advent of the 21st century. Partnering with Architectural Alliance on the new Guthrie Theatre, Nouvel and his Paris firm used the Alliance's offices near Loring Park as their headquarters.

Jean Nouvel

Tom D'Angelo, lead designer of the Guthrie for the Alliance, told me how working with Nouvel was different from that with other architects: "Nouvel doesn't sit down and start drawing as we Minnesotans do. He talks over ideas with French philosophers, artists, and others over lunch and wine, in the European tradition." The French architect stressed the cultural context of his work, sublimating any hint of classicism. While visiting Minneapolis, the Alliance team welcomed him, showed him the town's high spots, and in the evenings reveled with him and the French team in a spirit of joie de vivre.

One evening Tom Fisher, dean of the College of Design at the University of Minnesota, invited us to hear and meet Nouvel backstage at the old Northrop Auditorium. He seemed cordial enough but to us friendly Minnesotans he came off as haughty, perhaps because he didn't speak English well, which became apparent during his speech. Nouvel talked a lot about the river, the old mills, and how he envisioned the new theater as part of the neighborhood.

In 2006, the new Guthrie opened to a somewhat startled public. The big bold building, clad in midnight blue, housed three theaters—the thrust stage in a cylindrical shape, the proscenium theater in the rectangular east end, and a black-box studio theater, the Dowling Studio, hanging outside at Level 9. In some ways, the whole evoked the industrial feel of the old mills and their circular silos.

In other ways, it appeared to me to be a brand-new kind of architecture, a little foreboding yet curiously exciting. As a longtime Guthrie fan, I was eager to see the three theaters inside. Riding up the sky-high escalator was the first shock. And trying to find the appropriate theater was difficult, mainly because the crowd circulation was dreadful. But the Guthrie's "Endless Bridge," with its expansive views of the Mississippi River, the Stone Arch Bridge, and the converted mills, almost made up for that. I gathered that Nouvel had to make Level 4 serve as a lobby or crossroads, where the two main theaters intersect with the cantilevered bridge. The architect said, "The theater is a machine for capturing and radiating the enveloping vistas."

For those of us attending plays at new Guthrie, the productions are excellent, as ever, though we may spend some time finding our seats. Nouvel created a new and different kind of architecture, one that clearly attracts—or turns off—one viewer or another.

## Bill Pedersen

"A Minnesota Success Story—Bill Pedersen, One of America's Most Sought After Architects." Such was the headline of my 1990 story about Kohn Pedersen Fox (KPF), cofounded by Pedersen in New York City in 1976.

Admittedly, I'd come to know this modest architect personally, as he often visits his relatives in the Twin Cities. Pedersen was a key hockey player at the University of Minnesota, and to me he is still a Gopher at heart. As a proud graduate of the university's School of Architecture, he credits his former professor James Stageberg with giving him the confidence he needed to trade his hockey stick for a pencil. Pedersen also recognizes architect Leonard Parker, who hired him right after graduation and taught him "what it means to be an architect."

After gaining a master's degree at the Massachusetts Institute of Technology (MIT) and winning the Rome Prize, Pedersen landed a job in I. M. Pei's New York office. Then, with the mid-1970s recession, the bottom dropped out. Nevertheless, Pedersen met with Eugene Kohn and Sheldon Fox to forge a new enterprise in 1976.

Bill Pedersen

"We knew we had the capacity to be big," Pedersen said. They took the plunge and set about making KPF an architecture firm to reckon with.

KPF's first break came in the form of a project for the New York City studios of ABC-TV, the second a commission for a tower for AT&T in Virginia. Others followed, and in just 14 years, KPF set an incredible record of architectural achievement, winning the AIA's firm-of-the-year award for design excellence in 1990.

Following the receipt of that award Pedersen has concentrated on his earlier vision—the development of high-rise commercial buildings that conduct architectural conversation with the buildings around them. Today KPF's work graces the skylines of cities around the world, including the Twin Cities, in which four of Pedersen's commissioned buildings reside. The most recent is the University of Minnesota's Science Teaching and Student Services Center.

I have seen Pedersen's gracefully curving building—333 West Wacker Drive—in Chicago, the Gannet/*USA TODAY* Headquarters in Virginia, and his ultimate high-rise, the Shanghai World Financial Center. His use of modern technology with a nod to the classical makes this work a standout.

When Pedersen visited his hometown during construction of the Saint Paul Companies tower in 1989, he remarked: "This was the opportunity to form a great urban space—a triangle combining the Hamm Plaza and Landmark Center." The building of Cold Spring gray granite and Mankato stone carries the Pedersen stamp in its pyramidal roof, smaller-scale pavilions, and detailed window treatment.

Having just attended a 1990 ceremony at which he received the university's CALA Alumni Achievement Award, the athletic architect expressed some regret about giving up hockey to a student nearby. Then Pedersen grinned and admitted, "I've had a great time though."

## David Salmela, Minnesota's own

David Salmela

Dick Hammel, my architect husband, discovered a talented but unknown draftsman in northern Minnesota. Dick loved to design schools, and he took pride in the number of school districts he lined up for commissions. For him, the opening of a new school was a special joy. He loved seeing the response of young pupils and teachers to their new buildings. The firm built multiple schools for the Rosemount school district among others.

In the late 1970s Dick arranged a meeting with a Virginia, Minnesota firm, Damberg and Peck (now DSGW), helping to design a new middle school in Mountain Iron, Minnesota. He invited me to join him on the short trip north. The local firm's employees were excited to meet the "big-time" architect from the Twin Cities. As we toured the office, Dick stopped at a young man's drafting table and asked his name.

"David Salmela, and I'm not really an architect, just a draftsman," he said with a smile.

Dick took one look at his drawing and replied quietly, "You *are* an architect." Over lunch, we learned that Salmela had no formal architectural education but practiced as a licensed architect. Blessed with natural talent and a passion for architecture, he had learned by doing and continued working in the field.

After a few years, Salmela established his own office—Salmela Architect—in Duluth and began to design houses. Influenced by his Finnish-American background and rocky lake-filled environment, his work demonstrated a singular prowess for designing simple forms, interiors flooded with daylight, and the use of natural materials—usually wood painted white or later, black.

As Salmela's clients grew, so did the number of houses he designed. Soon they were winning awards from the Minnesota AIA. To date he has won some 45 awards, more than most Twin City designers. His 2000 design, with landscape architect Shane Coen, of the Jackson Meadow homes at Marine on the Saint Croix is a standout.

Salmela's reputation has spread nationally, even internationally, and the personable Finn is no longer considered just a regional architect. Nevertheless, many of his homes reflect the spirit of the northland via his use of rural forms such as barns and sheds. Modernism seems to be in his Scandinavian roots. Salmela describes his style as "early modernism." He has gone on to design industrial buildings such as the Hawks Boot factory in Duluth. I am especially smitten with his Izzy's Ice Cream factory, a small pink and white building with a "cherry" on top, to which Guthrie Theatre patrons can easily walk.

In 2008, Salmela was awarded the Minnesota AIA Gold Medal.

Tom Fisher in his book *The Invisible Element of Place: The Architecture of David Salmela* (University of Minnesota Press, 2011) says the architect was shocked when he heard the news: "I always thought the Gold Medal went to an architect towards the end of his career. I am just starting to learn things."

The starchitect stories largely draw from my work journals. The story about Bill Pedersen draws from my article "A Minnesota Success Story—Bill Pedersen, One of America's Most Sought After Architects," published in the June 1990 issue of *Minnesota Real Estate Journal.*

# 21 Egypt and Jordan 1989

We're going to Egypt, Bette!" exclaimed my good friend Jock Nolte Jones. I was stunned, but when I learned that her brother, former U.S. ambassador to Egypt Richard Nolte, would lead the tour, I knew we had to go. The trip was billed "A Visit to Egypt and Jordon via the Red Sea." It was two years after my husband's death, and I was raring to see some of the world's most ancient architecture.

As our plane approached the Red Sea port of Suez, we flew over the pyramids for a breathtaking view. I could hardly believe we were going to see this ancient land. We soon boarded a Greek cruise ship, carrying just 150 passengers, with the rest of the "Minnesota mafia." Dick Nolte was indeed our guide. He had lived in Cairo with his wife, Jean, for about two years when their stay ended with Egypt's Six-Day War with England. He was certain to know a lot about the country.

We sailed on the Red Sea to Safaga, Egypt, a barren-looking industrial/agricultural port, then boarded buses headed for Luxor through a moonscape of rocks and mountains. Luxor was a pretty town with greenery along the Nile River; there we stayed in a big old British colonial-style hotel. Nearby were the famed temples of Karnak.

The Great Sphinx and the Great Pyramid of Giza are among the Seven Wonders of the Ancient World.

If you've seen the Agatha Christie movie *Death on the Nile,* you may recall the huge columns of Karnak. The magnificent stone columns—134 of them standing and all inscribed—reached far above our heads. I was thrilled to see the columns as well as the great statues of King Ramses and the avenue of ram-headed sphinxes. As our local guide said, "Never has the art of architecture reached such great heights in any civilization."

The next site, requiring a short flight to Abu Simbel, was even more impressive. The government of Egypt, in an ingenious feat of modern technology, moved the colossal sculptures of King Ramses up and away from the threatening waters caused by construction of the High Dam to a site overlooking the manmade Lake Nasser. The statues, measuring to 60 feet in height, appear to have been there forever. Inside and out of the two temples there are carefully preserved wall inscriptions, hieroglyphics, and drawings depicting life in ancient times.

After visiting there, we quickly took in the Valley of the Kings and King Tut's tomb, eager to move on to the pyramids before heading for the Red Sea and through the Suez Canal to Cairo.

Cairo is a teeming city of millions of people, dust, traffic, and modern buildings alongside mosques, lacy minarets, and the city's Museum of Egyptian Antiquities. Our hotel was located in an area near the pyramids. We were shocked to see development built right to the foot of the Great Pyramid.

We were driven close enough to see the three pyramids that sit high on the Plateau of Giza and the desert stretching for miles beyond them. I marveled at how a civilization of 5,000 years ago accomplished such works. Our guide emphasized that farmers, not slaves, made all the bricks, while a master craftsman figured out how to lay them. The Great Sphinx, on the east side of the complex, was also a great wonder.

## Jordan

One of the world's most unforgettable architectural sites is the ancient city of Petra. To get there, we mounted horses led by native guides, then rode through a narrow gorge until the canyon walls almost seemed to close. Then, suddenly we caught sight of the Treasury, Corinthian columns and all, incredibly carved into the rock. The ancient Nabataeans, an Arabian tribe, built the entire city of Petra into the rough sandstone walls ranging in color from rose, pink, and yellow to blue.

With the guide, our group, my friend Jock Jones, and I toured the well-preserved city, including a library, Roman theater, museum, temples, and tombs. Some of us followed him on the high climb—over steep steps to the top of the cliffs carved into the mountainside (we took an easier trail coming down). I marveled again at how ancient civilizations were able to create such mind-boggling structures. I will never forget Petra.

Still in Jordan, we cruised up the Gulf of Aqaba slated to attend a Bedouin feast for lunch in the desert of the Wadi Rum, which the British officer T. E. Lawrence (Lawrence of Arabia) marched through with his Arabs. The scenery there was spectacular with red sandstone cliffs and desert stretching between them to a flat plain. Camel drivers greeted us and demonstrated how to mount the camels. We rode about two blocks into the encampment of the Bedouins—nomad Arabs still traveling the old routes with their goats and sheep. There, seated on Arabian rugs, we enjoyed one of the best lunches of our trip.

Before we left Jordan, the ship's cruise director announced that we would have a short time for shopping before departure. Aqaba is a bustling, fairly modern, port city, jam-packed with oil trucks and people. Naturally, Jock and I went exploring. We ventured into a shoe shop to buy sandals. The shopkeeper, a beaming young man, delighted at having American customers,

The spectacular desert of the Wadi Rum,
where Lawrence of Arabia led his Arabian forces to victory

especially my pretty friend Jock, brought her box after box of sandals for her to see. Looking for just the right thing, she followed him to the back of the shop. Suddenly, I heard a shriek, and Jock rushed out screaming, "He kissed me." The shopkeeper bowed and bowed, apologizing. After quickly paying for the sandals, we ran madly for the bus, knowing we were late.

The venture caused an international incident. That night, Jock innocently told her brother about the kiss, and Dick immediately reported it to the tourist police. The next day at the end of our Petra tour, the Aqaba police insisted on taking us off the ship to help locate the salesman, regardless that the ship was nearing departure. We were taken by taxi into the city, where Jock spotted the young man. He fled. The policeman explained that this kind of thing was unheard of in Jordan and they could not let it go unnoticed. We were whisked back to the ship, where a passengers and crew awaited us.

The young man escaped that day, but before long the local police chased down the unfortunate shopkeeper and arrested him. Jock and I felt sorry for him, but we agreed we would one day write a story about "The Kiss that Stopped the Ship."

This story draws from my travel journals.

# 22 Barcelona 1992

In a city famous for the swirls, squiggles, and flourishes of Antoni Gaudí's early 20th-century architecture, Ludwig Mies van der Rohe's Barcelona Pavilion in Spain is a beacon of its stark simplicity. While on a tour bus visiting Barcelona in 1992, I suddenly spotted the pavilion, realized we were not stopping, and shrieked in English, "Please let me out of here now." I had to see this masterpiece of international style.

Designed as Germany's entry for the 1929 Barcelona International Exposition, the sleek, rectangular structure of glass and marble was revolutionary for its time. Soon, the pavilion was dismantled and put in storage. Six decades later, the parts were found, and in 1986 it was faithfully reconstructed on the original site in honor of the 100th anniversary of the architect's birth.

Located on the lower slopes of Montjuïc (site of the Olympic games in 1992), the pavilion clearly illustrates Mies van der Rohe's mantra "less is more" with its interlocking linear planes of green marble, golden onyx, and gray-tinted glass. Clamp-like walls contain the space; slender steel columns support the flat roof. A long, low structure, it sits pristinely on a travertine podium overlooking a reflecting pool lined with black glass and holding perfectly matched stones.

Mies van der Rohe's famed pavilion, designed for
the 1929 Barcelona International Exposition,
now restored to its original simplicity

Mies van der Rohe designed a travertine bench alongside the pool to seat visitors enjoying their surroundings. An uninspired 1970s building blocks the view of the colorful Montjuïc, but tourists still can see the huge Palau Nacional, later restored to its late 1920s grandeur.

The pavilion's interior, channeling space between separate vertical and horizontal planes, is also a work of art. "It just flows," Ted Butler, HGA's design guru, told me. He was an ardent admirer of the pavilion from the time he was an architecture student at the University of Minnesota. Indeed, the interior spaces flow from one to another, leading to a small reflecting pool and a perfectly placed bronze sculpture of a nude by Georg Kolbe.

Mies van der Rohe also designed the pavilion's only furniture—two of his leather and chrome Barcelona chairs, originally meant to serve as thrones for the Spanish monarchy of the 1920s, King Don Alfonso XIII and Queen Victoria Eugenie.

In comparison to the neighboring complex of large-scale convention-style buildings used for Barcelona's many trade fairs, Mies van der Rohe's pavilion is minuscule yet inspiring. To see an original structure that changed the whole world of architecture was an exciting experience. The architect's concept was so far ahead of its time that the pavilion seemed designed for the century yet to come. Amid all the trappings of the 1992 Olympics, this elegant little building demonstrated the modernist's basic philosophy: A simple statement of form expresses order and truth.

## Other Barcelona "Musts"

As expected, Antoni Gaudí's exuberant architecture dominates this city. His works—including villas, apartments, churches, and parks—are hard to miss. With his lavish use of broken ceramic tile, whimsically shaped chimney caps, and elaborate curving façades, Gaudí could never stop "painting." Some say he was the Frank Gehry of his day. Clearly, Gaudí and his peers created a Catalan modernist style that took the international art nouveau movement to fanciful extreme.

Wandering around Barcelona via the metro, I found an important stop on Montjuïc—Fundació Joan Miró, a world-class example of modernism designed by Josep Louis Sert in the early 1970s. Miró's finest works are set off in a stunning white building accented with skylights and barrel-vaulted ceilings. Topping it all is a splendid roof garden, where some of Miró's sculpture is displayed. My friends and I had fun taking snapshots of each other among the pieces there.

My next museum stop—the Museu Picasso—was in the old Gothic or Bank Quarter. Pablo Picasso's early works and many

One of Antoni Gaudi's celebrated works, the Sagrada Familia Cathedral, with its many fanciful spires, was unfinished until recent years.

One of Gaudi's exuberant uses of concrete is a wall
that seems like waves on the exterior of the building La Pedrera.

more are displayed in five adjoining medieval stone palaces. (The courtyards alone are worth the visit.) Here you can trace the evolution of the artistic genius born in the city of Málaga in 1881. Though he spent only his formative years in Barcelona, the city ensured that much of Picasso's work is shown in a museum dedicated to him. It opened officially in 1983 with a collection of more than 4,000 works of art by Picasso.

In recent years, the museum added a new structure to alleviate crowding at the entrance.

---

This story draws from my article "Mies's Landmark Barcelona Pavilion Reconstructed," published in the September/October 1992 issue of *Architectural Record,* and another of mine in the July/August 1992 issue of *Active Lifestyles.*

# 23 Santa Fe 1997

The romantic southwestern town of Santa Fe beckoned ten of us Minnesota Preservation Alliance members and friends to the 51st annual conference of the National Trust for Historic Preservation (NTHP) in mid-October 1997. The National Preservation Conference, unusually popular that year, attracted almost 2,000 preservationists to the capital city of New Mexico.

Despite hosting so many tourists every year, Santa Fe is a charming, small (population about 68,000 in 1997) walkable city, unique in the United States in that all its architecture reflects its southwestern heritage. We loved the peach-and-sand-colored adobe buildings set against the bright sunny sky of New Mexico. We admired the farsighted planners of the 1920s, who set strict design architectural guidelines for what was then just another western town with the usual hodgepodge of building styles.

Originally the town was laid out around a central plaza. Over the years, only three architectural styles are reinforced and have prevailed: Spanish colonial, Pueblo revival (or a combination of the two), and territorial. Height is limited to five stories—hence the scale of the town is part of its magic. Accenting most of the adobe structures are wooden doors and windows, often painted blue or turquoise.

A visit to O'Keeffe's home:
The reddish-brown mountains of Ghost Ranch
are familiar subjects in the artist's paintings.

Former Minnesotan Richard Moe, then president of the National Trust, welcomed the crowd to the opening session, inviting members to enter into the conference theme that year: "People and Places: Living in Cultural Landscapes." The members then dispersed to see dozens of historic sites.

One of the most popular attractions—the Native American jewelry sale held on the sidewalk in front of the Palace of the Governors (a small museum of colonial and Native American history)—takes place in the central plaza of the city. A variety of colorful custom-made items designed by various Indian jewelry makers are always for sale. Items range from rings and bracelets to necklaces and earrings. Many are beaded or fashioned with silver and turquoise. Each piece is inspected for maker authenticity.

The biggest news for me at the conference was that of the NTHP's acquisition of Georgia O'Keeffe's home and studio. Earlier a property of the O'Keeffe Foundation, the home/studio was a new addition to the National Trust's collection of national historic sites.

Perched high on a mesa overlooking Abiquiú, a village 50 miles northwest of Santa Fe, O'Keeffe's home is a sprawling old adobe hacienda, remodeled by O'Keeffe in 1945. I was privileged to see it early—only the members of the press were allowed to visit there during the conference.

After reaching the top the mesa and parking well back from the site, I stood transfixed by the sweeping panorama before me. I could see the jagged purplish reddish-brown mountains to the west, the white cliffs of Ghost Ranch across the valley, and the yellow leaves of the cottonwood trees along the Chama River below. Suddenly I understood how much the natural environment had influenced the art of Georgia O'Keeffe. Back in Santa Fe the next day, I would recognize this landscape in the Georgia O'Keeffe Museum.

As visitors, we were not allowed to go inside the hacienda but

Santa Fe is built almost entirely of adobe, creating a homogeneous effect.

only to walk around the exterior and peer through picture windows to see how simply the artist lived for the last 35 years of her life. The furnishings of her home were 1950s modern. The windowsills were covered with small rocks (O'Keeffe was fascinated by shapes). The open patio was stark, with one door painted black. A Pueblo-style ladder leaned against a well. O'Keeffe's all-white studio faced north, commanding a great view.

Back in Santa Fe, the members of our group scattered through the town because there is so much art, craft, and architecture to see. The city features ten or more museums, including the Museum of International Folk Art, the Museum of Indian Arts and Culture, and a multitude of art galleries. No visitor should miss Canyon Road, the Palace of the Governors, or the 1966 New Mexico State Capitol, the only round state capitol in the United States. We learned much about the city's cultural heritage, how much the Spanish, the Navajo, and other Native Americans and their pueblos have influenced the city we see today.

My fellow preservationists and I were delighted to have made the trip to Santa Fe and recommend to all this singular, historic city in America's high-desert country.

This story draws from my article "Report from Santa Fe," published in the November, 1997 issue of *Preservation Matters* (a newsletter).

# 24 Vancouver 1997

One look at Seattle's busy waterfront lined with hundreds of boats on the sparkling waters of Puget Sound, and I was a goner. I just had to get on a ferryboat and head out to sea. Destination: Vancouver.

After a picturesque voyage with a stop at Victoria, on Vancouver Island, we landed at Tswwassen, where we boarded a bus. Within an hour we entered British Columbia's great seaport. The sun was just setting, but we could see the skyline of the inner city, a Manhattan of the North. With the Pacific waters its front yard, the city teems with high-rise towers against the backdrop of a majestic coastal mountain range. In contrast to Manhattan, Vancouver is a peninsula, not an island.

According to our local tour guide, Vancouver was witnessing phenomenal population growth in the late 1990s. Hence the dramatic increase in high-rise condominium towers, almost all with balconies.

After walking around the city, I could understand why so many people wanted to be there. Vancouver is a highly livable place, compact enough to get around easily, with many parks, beaches, and marinas. For example, Stanley Park, five minutes from downtown, contains 1,000 forested acres complete with beaches, open-air theater, aquarium, rowing, yacht clubs, and

Everyone has a balcony in this spectacular port city built with countless high-rise towers.

totem poles. Nearby mountains beckon to skiers, climbers, campers, and sailors.

First on our walking tour was the Port of Vancouver. Canada Place, built for Expo 1986 and jutting into Burrard Inlet, is the icon of Vancouver. The massive complex covers three city blocks. Easily identifiable from land or from sea, its five Teflon®-coated sails mark the place where cruise ships by the hundreds dock every year. Standing at the docks, I was mesmerized, amazed that such huge ships could even enter the city.

Among the newer works of architecture in Vancouver is a massive new library. Designed by (Mosha) Safdie Architects with Downs/Archambault (now DA Architects + Planners), the building reminds me of the Roman Coliseum. The largest capital project built by the city to date, the library is a powerful architectural statement. At first glance the structure appears to be circular though actually it is elliptical, with a nine-story glass box inside. Its façade appears to be rosy-brown stone, but it is precast concrete made from locally quarried granite.

Entering the library, I was delighted to see a six-story atrium soaring above the lively pedestrian street. Reading rooms are stashed in the freestanding columnar wall. Back of the library, completed in 1995, the architects attached a 22-story government office tower.

Next I was off to see an Arthur Erickson masterpiece, Vancouver's Museum of Anthropology, a stunning building of the 1960s. Passing through its carved door toward the Great Hall, I stood in admiration before the west façade, a 45-foot-high glass wall framing several towering totem poles and a massive contemporary carving of a giant raven. Daylighting throughout makes it easy to see the fascinating art of the First Nations people of the Pacific Northwest.

On the edge of the University of British Columbia campus, the glass-and-concrete museum overlooks the Strait of Georgia.

A massive library designed by Canadian world-prize winner Mosha Safdie Architects shows imaginative use of space and a form resembling the Roman Coliseum.

Outside, a walkway leads to traditional Haida houses, more fierce totem poles, and a beautiful view of mountains and sea.

Back to downtown Vancouver, we saw another award-winning Erickson work, his 1979 Law Courts Building, identifiable by its sloping glass roof. Further down the hilly street is the city's historic district—Gastown—featuring a restored warehouse area and cobblestone streets. Much of it reminded me of the Warehouse District in Minneapolis.

On Vancouver's south end, Granville Island is the gem. Once an industrial wasteland, it is now a popular gathering place, with a farmers market, art galleries and studios, waterfront restaurants, and boats galore. Granville is a prime example of urban renewal with a festive flair.

All too soon it was time for me to return to Seattle for the flight home. But before I left, I got my wish to see an ocean liner close up. The *Nieuw Amsterdam* was docked alongside Canada Place. As I joined those admiring the ship, I imagined being on board, pulling away from Vancouver into the Pacific for another architectural adventure.

This story draws on my article "Vancouver Is an Urban Frontier with Nature as Its Backdrop," published in the January/February 1997 issue of *Architecture Minnesota.*

# 25 London Plus 1998

Of all the great cities across the Atlantic, none appeals to me more than London. The city has called to me to visit at least three times.

In 1997, an enviable invitation arrived—two tickets to Wimbledon, thanks to my niece Anne Person Worcester of Connecticut, the first CEO of the Women's Tennis Association. In response, a tennis friend and I were quickly London-bound.

At the time, architects were busily designing new modern buildings or converting older ones in London. The new/old building that I intended to see was the 1997 version of Shakespeare's Globe Theatre.

## The Globe Theatre

Located on the south banks of the Thames, the new Globe takes the visitor a step back in time. Shakespeare's language comes to life without the benefit of sets, props, or high-tech lighting in this 1997 replica of the 1599 original. With standing-room tickets procured at the last minute, my friend and I were fortunate to experience a Globe production of *Henry V* in June, shortly after the theatre opened.

And it *was* an experience. I was so carried away by the

The new Globe Theatre was built much like
Shakespeare's original, of ground white limestone with timber trim.

authenticity of the set and the powerful acting that I could visualize English troops crossing the channel only to be cut down by the French, the king agonizing over the bloody conflict.

This is theatre the way Shakespeare himself staged it. Roof-covered bleachers with backless seats surround an open-pit area flanking the stage, allowing standees to be close to the action. When we grew tired of standing, we leaned against the nearest bleacher railing.

The circular stage, topped with a thatched roof, projects into the semicircular roofless area, supported by two marbled wood columns with gilded capitals. The actors, in rich and colorful Shakespearean costume, entered through a curtain at the back. Overhead, from a balcony, three trumpeters announced the entrance of the king.

It's easy to spot the Globe from pedestrian walkways along the River Thames. At first glance, the theatre's exterior resembles white stucco with timber trim. We soon learned that the exterior coating is ground limestone mixed with goat hair. The polygon-shaped theatre structure is of English oak, right up to its thatched roof. Modern amenities including restrooms and a coffee bar are available in an adjoining brick building connected to the theatre via a covered walkway or an outdoor plaza.

No wonder critics have called the new Globe a remarkable reconstruction of Shakespeare's 1599 original.

## Wimbledon

Clutching our two-day tickets, tennis friend Peggy Watson and I excitedly took the tube to the suburb of Wimbledon after getting directions from a friendly Englishman. The championship tournament has been held in this same place since 1877, when it was called the "All England Lawn Tennis and Croquet Club." Wimbledon is the only Grand Slam tennis tournament still played on a traditional grass court.

We found Wimbledon to be a vast complex encompassing two major, partially roofed stadiums, countless green-grass outdoor courts with bleachers, huge scoreboards, and assorted pavilions. At the entry we saw row upon row of festive, green-and-white-striped tents. On a grassy hillside, purple and white petunias adorned a picnic area. Strawberries with cream or frozen yogurt, accompanied by champagne or tea and crumpets, was the order of the day in the tea pavilion.

Our seats for the game were in historic Centre Court, originally opened in 1922. Recently remodeled, the oval-shaped open-air stadium with a sweeping new roof holds more than 13,000 fans, a new box for the royals, and improved broadcast booths.

Nearby is Wimbledon's newest stadium, No. 1 Court, accommodating 11,400 followers. Watching such stars as Michael Chag and Arantxa Sanchez-Vicario was exciting, but experiencing Wimbledon was the real thrill. As English journalist Simon Barnes has written, "It is not the strawberries that make Wimbledon great. Wimbledon happens to be one of the finest theatres of sport in the world."

## The Isle of Wight

It was a rainy week in London, and I was beginning to long for the sea and sunshine. Since the Isle of Wight is known for its coastal walks, yacht harbors, and beaches, we decided to venture there for the last two days of our trip. The journey meant taking a train south to Portsmouth, a ferry to the island, and a short train-and-bus ride to the south-coast town of Ventnor, touted as Queen Victoria's favorite escape and for its great views of the sea.

As the rain seemed abating, we stepped cautiously from our B&B at the top of the steep hill we had climbed, toting our luggage. A kind neighbor spotted us and offered his help, which we gladly accepted. After a little tea, we learned he was a retired tour guide. Gathering we were disappointed by the weather, he promptly offered to drive us around "his" island.

Thanks to the retired tour guide, we took in the thatched cottages of Calbourne village, sampled a short coastal walk on the top of the downs, lunched near the Needles (chalky white perpendicular cliffs), explored Tennyson Down where Alfred Lord Tennyson lived and wrote, and visited Carisbrooke Castle and the busy harbor of Yarmouth. Authors Charles Dickens, Lewis Carroll, and John Keats, also inspired by the beauty of the isle, lived there too.

Members of the British royalty enjoyed the Isle of Wight as well: Queen Victoria and her Prince Albert spent some time

Queen Victoria loved her home, Osborne House on the Isle of Wight, where she lived for many years with her beloved Prince Albert.

there in her home known as Osborne House. It appears to be a brick mansion, surrounded by lush gardens and overlooking the sea. When the queen first saw it, she said, "It's hard to imagine a prettier spot." She must have loved her time with her husband there, as she couldn't bear to leave the isle after Prince Albert's death. She spent many years grieving him on Wight.

It was as hard for me to leave the Isle of Wight whence, high on the downs, I could look over the English Channel and dream of sailing to France.

This story draws from my travel journals and from my article "A Visit to the Globe Theatre, Wimbledon, and the Isle of Wight," published in the January/February 1998 issue of *Architecture Minnesota.*

# 26 Chicago, Revisited

The windy city, the big bold brash city, the city where all architecture fans love to go! It's not just the great skyline but also the history of the city. And the architects who built the city—Louis Sullivan, Daniel Burnham, Mies van der Rohe, and all who followed—are enough to make us giddy.

For many years, I toured Chicago's latest architectural triumphs thanks to Dick Hammel's boyhood friend from Owatonna, Minnesota—Donald Rowley, M.D., a distinguished researcher at the University of Chicago. His remarkable wife—Janet Davison Rowley, M.D., a U of C researcher who made a renowned discovery in her work with cancer cells—joined us on our tours.

The Rowleys lived in Hyde Park, a neighborhood within easy bike ride of the university campus, in a three-story 1920s craftsman style house, once the home of Chicago's chief of police. They were also architecture buffs, and in an effort to educate me on Frank Lloyd Wright, they took me on an early trip to see the Frederick C. Robie House adjacent to the university.

Built in 1903, this old house is one of the most famous homes in the United States. Naturally I was eager to tour my first Prairie Style house (Louis Sullivan coined the style name). Soon I readily understood why the style had become so popular.

The entrance of the Robie house was somewhat hidden, but I could see at once how the long low stretch of the structure

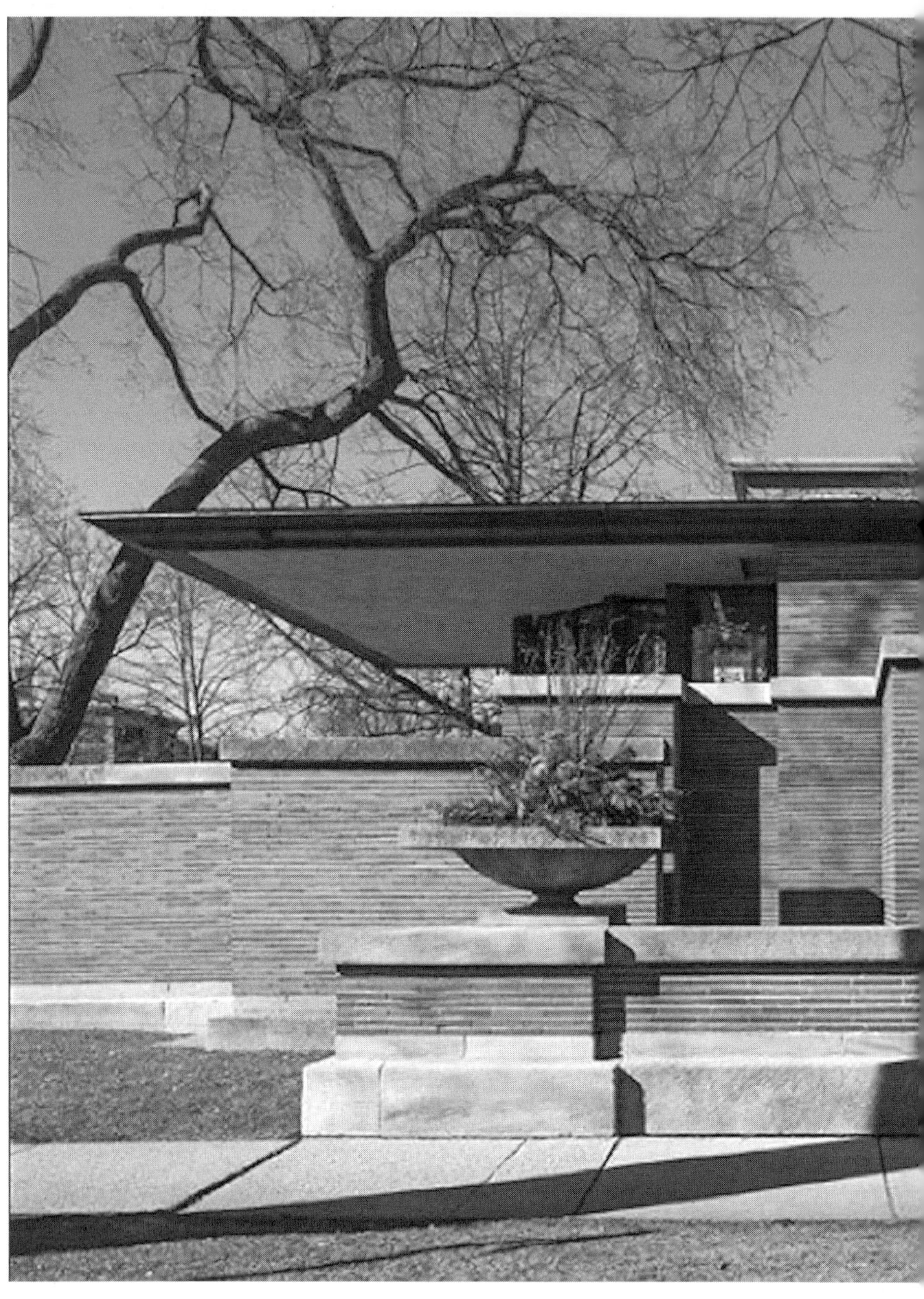

The long, low structure of Frank Lloyd Wright's Robie House, 1903, exemplifies his Prairie Style, which captivated homeowners across the United States.

conveys the vast land of the Midwest. The brick and concrete house is formed of two parallelogram-shaped sections with a small third structure on top. It certainly was unlike any house I had ever been in. Unique, intriguing, and massive, it was not in any way ostentatious in the way that our modern McMansions hover grandly over their sites.

Heavy cantilevered overhangs shaded the interior of the Robie house from the sun. The exterior trim was of thin Roman brick and limestone. Inside, the floors were of reinforced concrete. The furnishings, designed by Wright, were rather ponderous. I loved the windows and doors, many hung with leaded and stained glass. The main floor space was divided not by walls but by horizontal detailing, a form of early modernism.

The best way to see Chicago, according to Janet Rowley, was to take a Chicago River cruise. And she was so right! Docents from the Chicago Architecture Foundation lead these tours, and I learned a lot.

I boarded one of the boats below the Michigan Avenue Bridge (officially the DuSable Bridge). As we headed out, everyone gasped at the beauty of the all-white, Spanish revival-style Wrigley Building, its tiled façade glittering in the sun. Charles G. Beersman designed this gem, constructed from 1919 to 1924. Not far away stands another Chicago symbol, the neo-gothic Tribune Tower, its 36 stories clad in Indiana limestone, built from 1923 to 1925. New York's John Mead Howells and Raymond Hood designed it.

Next we approached Marina City, providing a great view of how people live, work, and play in that ever-spiraling environment. Architect Bertrand Goldberg gave Chicagoans something to talk about with his two apartment buildings of pie-shaped loops and round, cast-concrete forms rising one after another. Built from 1959 to 1967, the complex is known as a "city within a city." In comparison, the bulky Chicago Merchandise Mart, which we passed next, seemed like a gigantic warehouse.

We caught a glimpse of the semicircular State of Illinois Center, renamed the James R. Thompson Center, rising 17 stories on the other side of the river over a glitzy glass atrium of pink and blue, designed by Murphy/Jahn Architects. Later on a land tour, I walked through that building and wondered why Helmut Jahn was so overcome by postmodernism. Compared to his ingenious design of the United Airlines Terminal 1, at O'Hare International Airport, this building seems unworthy of his talent.

Earlier, because of Jahn's stellar reputation, some of us attending the 1980 National AIA Convention had wished to visit his office, and we did. His firm's offices were located in the Jewelers' Building, an early Adler & Sullivan building. It is a relatively small high-rise (12 floors), noted for its Louis Sullivan decoration. The big thrill of that tour was walking out on the top-floor, open-air plaza and looking down on the great city, its lights glimmering through the misty night . . .

Continuing the river tour around the next bend, I spotted Bill Pedersen's 333 West Wacker Drive tower of 36 stories, its green-glass façade echoing the curve of the river. This widely acclaimed building gave KPF its national reputation for designing and building skyscrapers.

All along the cruise was a passing host of significant architecture, including that of a bold new skyscraper, the 2009 International Trump Tower and Hotel and, later, two historic buildings—the 1929 Civic Opera House and the grand, old Chicago Union Station. Finally at the climax of the tour, we looked skyward at the most famous skyscraper of all—the Sears Tower, now the Willis. Over the years, I have visited that tower at least two or three times, just for the thrill of whizzing to the top and Skydeck Chicago, 103 stories up. There I gasp at how the structural engineers accomplished this wonder for architect Skidmore, Owings & Merrill (SOM).

As a preservationist, one of my favorite walking tours was a

Aboard a Chicago riverboat, we passed State Street Bridge and Marina City—Goldberg's rounded tower of concrete loops. The Wrigley building is visible in the distance.

loop tour, on which I took in the Rookery Building to understand how Chicago's architecture looked at the turn of the century. Designed in 1885 by Burnham & Root using both masonry and steel-frame construction, it was one of the first modern skyscrapers with an indoor court bringing in the sunlight. Frank Lloyd Wright renovated the lobby and court, eliminating some ironwork and adding marble scored with geometric patterns detailed in gold leaf. The result is a beautifully lacy effect on the curving stairways. Fortunately for us, Wright's 1907 design has been preserved.

Other buildings of the early Chicago School I admire include the Monadnock Building by Burnham & Root, 1891, the last and tallest skyscraper with masonry loadbearing walls, 17 stories. On State Street, the Reliance Building is considered the first-ever glass-and-steel skyscraper. Daniel Burnham and John Root also designed the Reliance, but after John Root's death in 1891, another firm member, Charles B. Atwood, continued. The building was completed in 1895. The Reliance is famous for its balance of huge picture windows with double-hung window and its placement of bay windows away from its frame so as to hide its columns. After more recent renovation, it is the attractive, modern Hotel Burnham.

During the 1980 AIA convention, I also toured the Chicago Board of Trade Building, another historic and elegant structure by Holabird & Root. Built in 1930, the 45-story tower is outstanding for its jagged art deco design and pyramidal roof. Even more intriguing is the 1980 addition designed by Murphy/Jahn and others of two setbacks. One is a spectacular atrium, and the other is built of steel and glass combined with the original limestone exterior.

Of all the Chicago skyscrapers I've explored, my favorite is still John Hancock Center, a 1970 masterpiece by architect Bruce Graham of SOM. I love the way its structure is expressed by the

The John Hancock Center by SOM, 1970, with its truncated obelisk design, is still my favorite of Chicago's many skyscrapers.

Gothic towers abound on the University of Chicago campus, founded in 1890. The towers frame the quads there, much as at Oxford and Cambridge.

gigantic, black anodized-aluminum X's soaring to 1,127 feet. It has been described as a truncated obelisk, and indeed I could feel its slope as the elevator ascended.

As Ada Louise Huxtable once wrote, "The most beautiful skyscrapers are not only big, they are bold." The Hancock symbolizes the powerful boldness of this city, and yet it contains homes, restaurants, shops, and art. Reaching the top and seeing Lake Michigan sparkling before me, I thought, and I still think, the Hancock is the best modernist tower of them all.

As the widow of a modernist architect, I had to see examples of Ludvig Mies van der Rohe's work in Chicago. During the 2008 AIA National Convention, Donald Rowley drove me to inspect the Illinois Institute of Technology (IIT) College of Architecture building—S. R. Crown Hall—a bit more than two miles southwest of McCormick Place. It was spare, singular, and refined, basically a glass box floating between two translucent concrete frames. At its dedication in 1956, Mies said, "Let this building be the home of ideas and adventure."

Also on my list were his two glass-and-steel apartment buildings on North Shore Drive, which have influenced so much of modern architecture. Even so, many of today's glass boxes do not display the refinement of Mies's originals. What set the originals apart? Was it his use of I beams as mullions? Ultimately, the steel-and-glass exteriors became known as "curtain walls" and Mies's hallmark. For the modernist architects I knew, Mies van der Rohe was the inspiration. Is it any wonder Chicago is at the top of my list for original modernism?

One of my fondest memories of Chicago is walking through the quads of the University of Chicago. The campus goes back to 1891, and its gothic forms immediately bring to mind the English settings of Oxford and Cambridge. I loved wandering through the quads, especially beautiful with springtime tulips and daffodils. Henry Lee Cobb designed the quads and most of the buildings. His plan consisted of six broken quadrangles with gothic academic buildings on adjacent streets.

As the university and its campus expanded, its architecture gradually reflected early modernism. Now it is more contemporary, and it prompts the memory of my dear departed friends, the Doctors Rowley. They would be so happy to know that Barack Obama's presidential library will grace the University of Chicago campus, a grand salute to the teachers and students who have made it famous.

This story draws from my personal experience with the Rowleys, with some reference to *The AIA Guide to Chicago* by Alice Sinkevitch (New York: Mariner Books, 1993, PDF available online); *Why Architecture Matters: Lessons from Chicago* by Blair Kamin (Chicago: University of Chicago Press, 2001); and *Chicago by* Fodor's Travel (New York: Fodor's, 2014).

# 27 Dubrovnik 2000

As our 43-foot rental yacht searched a mooring in the tiny Croatian hamlet of Kobas, a tall young man spotting the American flag waved from the stern halyard, then dashed to the dock, shouting "Americans! Ladies!"

Wherever we navigated along the Dalmatian coast of Croatia, we American women sailors created quite a stir. It was obvious the Croatians and other crews, mostly from Austria and Germany, had rarely seen an all-female crew, especially one made up of six blondes from Minnesota.

It was year 2000, not long after the Bosnian War. My intrepid writer/sailor friend Carol Pine, through a magazine assignment, had discovered the joys of sailing the beautiful Dalmatian coast the year before. After seeing her photos, we clamored to join her for a similar trip the next spring. Ever since my school days in South Saint Paul, where Yugoslavians were my friends, I had dreamed of seeing Dubrovnik, the romantic site described by the English poet Lord Byron as "the Pearl of the Adriatic." Now was my chance.

I knew Dubrovnik had been severely damaged in 1991, but I was determined to learn more. Thanks to the local Croatian consulate in Saint Paul, I met a young woman from Dubrovnik, a native Croatian whose father was a contractor for that city's

Carol Pine, writer and sailor of distinction, led an all-female crew on a voyage through the Croatian Islands, headed for Dubrovnik.

restoration. Eureka! I knew I had the makings of a great story. In a short time, I landed an assignment with *Architectural Record* to write about "The Restoration of Dubrovnik." I began lining up dates for interviews.

We began our voyage at Trogir in Split-Dalmatia County, Croatia. Its collection of Romanesque and Renaissance-style architecture, dating to the 13th century, was impressive.

As we continued our trip, I came to realize that all these islands were built up with medieval architecture from the time of Marco Polo. From Hvar to Korčula, I admired picturesque harbors, gothic palaces, streets paved with creamy polished stone like that of the U.S. White House, artistically carved stone ornamentation, ancient buildings with high turrets, fragrant lavender spilling over the sloped highlands, and even Russian-designed marinas.

The skipper timed our arrival in Dubrovnik perfectly, for early afternoon after four days of sailing, just before the appointed time for my interview with the local contractor.

With a friend serving as my photographer, I took a cab through the high, winding streets to meet Marko Kovačević, CEO of GP Dubrovnik, whose firm hand handled the bulk of Dubrovnik's restoration projects. With an interpreter standing by I was able to conduct the interview—for the first time in my life I felt like a foreign correspondent!

Downhill from his office, we got our first glimpse of the red-tiled roofs of the walled city. It was a thrill to view this historic place, perched as it was on a spectacular site overlooking the Mediterranean Sea, which merges with the Adriatic nearby. Crossing the drawbridge into the old city was like entering the pages of ancient history. We passed through a massive archway to step down into a city built entirely of cream-colored stone with a glorious patina. We could barely surmise where the damage of the war had occurred. Since Dubrovnik evolved as an aristocratic republic from the 12th to the 19th centuries and then suffered devastating earthquakes, it bears the mark of architectural styles from Italian renaissance to gothic to baroque.

My next interview was with the president of the Association of Croatian Architects in Dubrovnik, architect Matko Vetma. He described the damage suffered by the city during the fall 1991 bombardment of Serb and Montenegrin forces of the Yugoslav National (or People's) Army. More than 2,000 shells damaged 68 percent of the old city's 824 buildings. Nine 17th-century palaces were gutted, 60 percent of the tiled roofs were destroyed.

Several European countries offered technical support for the renovation. Our contractor friend explained that it was difficult to get original tiles (*kupa*) because they were handmade. Looking down on the tiled roof, the tiles (including some new ones) appear to be from an old master's painting—some honey-colored and brownish, some burnished red, others varying from rosy to ochre.

The best way to see the city is to walk on top of the walls surrounding it. From there, we savored the dramatic vista of the sunlit Mediterranean and admired the old palaces, churches, and monasteries,. The stone houses reached five stories up among the spires and dome and an endless stretch of red-tile roofs. We noted many architectural influences—Greek and Roman to Austrian and Venetian.

Heading the restoration effort was Vjekoslav Vierda, director of the Institute for the Restoration of Dubrovnik. Only natural materials—stone, wood, and tile, no stucco—were used. Given the massive earthquake there in 1979, the city already had documented preservation guidelines. These provided the advisors the basis for developing a master plan.

The first priority was to repair the tall stone buildings housing most of the local residents. The priorities of the *United Nations Educational, Scientific and Cultural Organization* (UNESCO) included restoration of the oldest harbor city walls, a costly effort

The majority of mostly blond crew members had sailed with Carol Pine earlier, and they knew what a skilled skipper she was, whether on local, national, or international waters.

The Minnesota crew, including the author, often enjoyed taking a turn at the wheel.

requiring about three years of work. With the high return of tourism, the effort was well worth it.

Sailing back to Trogir, past other historic islands and harbors, we decided to enjoy the simple pleasures of Croatia—the delicious local wines, and freshly caught fish grilled to perfection . . . But wait a minute! Just as we were leaving Dubrovnik, I felt a compelling need to swim in the sparkling blue waters. The channel felt peaceful enough that the skipper said, "Okay, jump in Bette."

I dove in, with the rest of the crew watching for my safety. The water felt great. At first, I practiced a relaxed crawl, thinking I could easily keep up with the boat. Very soon, however, I realized that although the boat was moving slowly, I was struggling through a current and not going anywhere. I shouted "Wait! Wait!"

At once, Carol Pine turned the boat around, and the others threw me a line. As I climbed safely aboard, they laughed and shouted, "You've got to get back to Minnesota with your story, Bette." That final swim was my good-bye to Dubrovnik and one of my greatest adventures.

This story draws from my article "After the War: The Ancient City of Dubrovnik Comes Back" in the *Correspondent's File* section of the August 2000 issue of *Architectural Record.*

# 28 Istanbul 2001

Two hardworking architects, Nedret and Mark Butler, who base their offices in Istanbul, Turkey, have kept in touch with me since their graduation from the University of Minnesota School of Architecture and Nedret's landing a post at HGA in Minneapolis. After she learned about property inherited at home in Turkey, the Butlers returned there to establish their own business. In Istanbul, they remodeled a former alcohol (used in making *raki*, the national drink) factory for their offices.

Fast forward to year 2000. As soon as I signed up for a tour to Turkey with an Edina group, I contacted the Butlers. Learning that the tour would approach Istanbul via the Bosphorus, the Butlers planned to watch our watercraft from a window of their offices overlooking the strait. I would direct the boat pilot to head to the left on our approach. It worked! We waved madly back and forth, with most of the tour group joining in.

After I visited their home in Istanbul, Nedret set up a day of tours and interviews with the latest tower developer and architect of Istanbul. As a result, I wrote "Istanbul: Where Sultans' Palaces Meet New Architecture."

With domed mosques, tapering minarets, majestic Ottoman palaces, and magnificent site at the confluence of the Turkish Straits, Istanbul has become famous through the ages as the

With its ever-increasing population, Istanbul is rapidly becoming an ultramodern city offering high-rise towers for retail and business.

crossroads of civilization. Today, its romantic history confronts architects with increasing challenges as they struggle to blend shiny new office towers with buildings of the past. Compounding these problems are the ever-growing masses—13 million (now 14.6 million) people live in Istanbul.

"It's not easy to have a master plan where there are 500 people moving in every day," said architect Doğan Hasol, then editor at *YAPI* magazine and later president of the Turkish Architectural Foundation. "We have good architects and bad architecture. The problem is [that] the city is very large and very populated, so we don't have consistent plans, and the land is often occupied illegally. This situation causes big problems for good architects."

Hasol said most new buildings should be kept at the edge of the city or built around Istanbul's three architectural zones. In the old city, where a master plan restricts building heights, the Blue (Sultan Ahmed) Mosque, Hagia Sophia, and Topkapi Palace still stand as works of centuries-old architecture. But "no plan exists in the Golden Horn—the old harbor—in the main European district. In this area, we made mistakes, building high-rises behind palaces. Istanbul has some good examples of contemporary architecture, but they are spotty."

Most of the new towers cluster in a skyscraper district located off two major highways and a busy thoroughfare. One complex, completed in August 2000, is owned by Isbank (Türkiye *İş* Bankasi), one of Turkey's oldest and largest financial institutions. Occupying 2.3million square feet, the complex stands out for its distinctive Western-style contemporary design. Designed by the New York firm Swanke Hayden Connell Architects (SHCA), the $150-million complex consists of three similar towers on a four-story granite base.

Isbank Tower 1, at 50 stories the tallest, is the bank's main headquarters. From the 41st floor up, the biggest tower steps back in a zigzag sawtooth. One of two matching 34-story towers is owned by a bank holding company, Sise Cam. The third tower is leased to several companies. Constructed of blue insulating glass with aluminum frame and stainless steel bands at parapet level, the Isbank complex stands out on Istanbul's skyline.

SHCA principal architect Altan Gursel admitted that while the firm was excited about working with the client, there are difficulties in working in Turkey. Project architect Anandi Dutta, who worked closely with the contractor, Tepe Construction, insisted on American standards for construction. Because Istanbul is located in Turkey's earthquake zone, special consideration was given to up-to-date seismic design for the tower's structure, curtain wall, and granite application.

Since the 1999 and following catastrophic Turkish earthquakes, which heavily damaged poorly built housing developments on the outskirts of the city, quality housing has become a critical architectural issue in burgeoning Istanbul. With the establishment of new government regulations for structural design, the ban on building in the earthquake zone was lifted last fall.

Hasol said homes were previously built on loose soil without proper structural knowledge. Now the government is constructing many new houses and opening up a bidding process. People are living in temporary housing or tents while architects work furiously on plans for affordable housing.

Turkey has more than 35,000 architects, nearly 12,000 of them in Istanbul alone. Those working privately must be members of the Chamber of Architects of Turkey, while those employed by the government do not. The chamber is primarily a registration office, not a professional organization like the American Institute of Architects, but its members are striving to establish an AIA equivalent.

Today Istanbul is a modern city in every way. Like other cities of its size, it debates at length the merits of a new subway system, new bridges, more stadiums. Undoubtedly, a steady stream of

In 2003 architects Nedret and Mark Butler opened on the shores of the Bosphorus, their crowning achievement—the five-star hotel Sumahan on the Water.

high-rise construction will continue. Let's hope that planners retain and enhance the past of this majestic city while pursuing the new.

The Butlers, through their firm, M&N Butler Mimarlar, Ltd., designed and built a luxury hotel on their property on the Bosphorus. Hotel Sumahan on the Water and its restaurant opened to acclaim in 2005. The two retired from their practice to manage their glamorous hotel. In 2012 the Butlers opened a new restaurant, the Tapasuma, and the next year they founded a Study Abroad campus for design students from the University of Minnesota in Istanbul.

As to the current architecture in Istanbul, they say, "There are now many, many towers plus thousands of shopping malls. Looking downtown to the European side of the Bosphorus, it looks like Manhattan." As of 2014, there were about 50,000 registered architects in Turkey, 14,000 of them in Istanbul. More and more often, the new multiuse towers are designed by Turkish architects and built by Turkish developers.

This story draws from my article "Istanbul: Where Sultans' Palaces Meet New Architecture," published in the January 2001 issue of *Architectural Record.*

# 29 Calatrava, in Milwaukee and Valencia 2001–2003

The Spanish architect, Santiago Calatrava.

The Spanish architect Santiago Calatrava was one I didn't know until exciting news came to me from Milwaukee in 2001. Santiago Calatrava's newly opened addition for the Milwaukee Art Museum had just been pronounced an architectural icon. The reason? The winglike steel arms, the *Burke Brise Soleil,* that open and close the museum's new entry at specified times and also protect the glass roof over the entrance hall. With Lake Michigan the backdrop of the museum, the arms reminded me of sails gently moving with the breeze.

I drove with friends from Minneapolis to Milwaukee expressly to see this work and was completely smitten with Calatrava's architecture, a combination of engineering, artistry, and sculpture. A suspension bridge led us into the Quadracci Pavilion addition. The huge pavilion has a vaulted glass ceiling and features various sculptural pieces. Intended as a gathering space overlooking the lake, this postmodern architecture is a

Milwaukee acquired a brilliant architectural icon
when Calatrava designed huge steel wings that open
and close at the entry of the city's newly remodeled art museum.

A beautifully landscaped walkway bordered with
Calatrava's metal detailing leads to the City of Arts and Sciences.

counterpoint to the modernist War Memorial Center designed in 1957 as an arts center and veterans' memorial by Eero Saarinen.

Calatrava's design for the museum was his first work in the United States. I had to go abroad to see his other projects. Fortunately for me, an alert Milwaukee travel agent, Karen Bergenthal of Tours 'd Art, announced a tour to Portugal and Spain, mainly to see his work. In the fall of 2002, we took off.

Valencia, Spain, Calatrava's birthplace, was the highlight of the tour. Calatrava's (with Félix Candela) City of Arts and Sciences, an entertainment-based cultural and architectural complex, was still under construction in an old riverbed as the edge of the city. At first glimpse of the two completed buildings, I was awestruck—we had just entered the world of the future. This amazing architecture was unlike any I had ever seen combining sculpture engineering, and art forms.

Two buildings were open for touring. The *L'Hemisfèric*—a half-sphere composed of concrete—reminded me of a giant eye with an eyelid that opened and closed, from the inside revealing the pool surrounding the structure. The eye fully open exposed a dome for the IMAX theater.

The other building, the Museu de les Ciències Príncipe Felipe (Prince Felipe Science Museum), was taller and presented a skeletal image of hundreds of white steel rods crisscrossing each other through the space. The site included a finished aquarium, Europe's largest. We ate dinner seated next to walls of water filled with colorful fish. Now the City of Arts and Sciences includes the opera house and performing arts center under construction at that time.

When we had finished our oohing-and-aahing and were preparing to leave, our group entered an elevated pedestrian walkway. It was beautifully landscaped with palm trees, huge colorful plantings, and fascinating sculpture. Visiting all these imaginative architectural works was a dizzying, never-to-be-forgotten experience.

I never had the chance to meet Calatrava, but Minneapolis architect Ed Kodet, a member of the National Board of Directors of the AIA, visited him in his New York studio in preparation for the AIA Gold Medal Calatrava won in 2005.

Kodet said, "He was the most gracious, easygoing, friendly architect I have ever met."

This story draws from my travel journals.

# 30 Hometown Saint Paul

Coming home after a long trip is always gratifying, especially now that my daughter Susan, her husband Dan, and two enterprising teenagers—Caleigh and Danny—now live nearby. Although I've lived in Wayzata for many years and I enjoy being near Lake Minnetonka, coming home really means returning to my birthplace—Saint Paul, the historic river city of majestic domes pitched high above the bluffs of the Mississippi.

I love the golden horses of the Minnesota State Capitol gleaming in the sunlight, announcing the importance of the building on which they stand to all the state. I know well the three bridges of Saint Paul—Robert Street, Wabasha, and the High Bridge—outstanding architectural works in themselves.

In the heart of the city—a previously thriving retail center now bustling with popular restaurants, lies Rice Park, one of the most beautiful in the Twin Cities. It is just the right scale to offset the landmark architecture surrounding it. Those buildings reflect four different eras:

- Saint Paul Hotel, built in1910
- George Latimer Central Library, built in 1917 and remodeled in 2002
- Ordway Center for the Performing Arts, built in 1985, its Ordway Concert Hall in 2015
- Landmark Center, built 1892–1902 and restored 1972–1978

LANDMARK

Saint Paul's venerable Landmark Center dominates the city's charming Rice Park, an all-seasons delight.

In summer, people flock to Rice Park to relax on benches in the shade of the trees along several paths. In warmer times, they might watch teenagers parading their finery on prom night or children giggling at the fountain. They might stroll the park, stopping to admire the statue of F. Scott Fitzgerald or bronze versions of Charlie Schulz's *Peanuts* characters. In winter, Rice Park sparkles with a thousand lights and ice sculptures viewed comfortably from the mezzanine of the glamorous Ordway Center for the Performing Arts.

Up Cathedral Hill, visitors may tour historic exhibits inside the monumental Minnesota History Center, a work of Minnesota limestone and granite designed by Bruce Abrahamson of HGA in 1973. Outside the Great Hall is a terrace providing an all-encompassing view of the city below. The third floor of the center, a wide corridor featuring a vaulted oak ceiling, offers such a splendid view of the Minnesota State Capitol that many couples choose to marry there.

The Minnesota State Capitol was designed by Cass Gilbert, who later became known for his work in New York. After more than a century, the building needed extensive restoration, which began in 2014.

Each time I visit the capitol, I remember the first time I climbed the marble steps leading to the Senate floor. I was just a teenager, but I knew one of the legislators, who found me a seat in the visitors' gallery. I still marvel at how architect Cass Gilbert accomplished the artistic, stately building now undergoing massive restoration.

Following Dick Hammel's death in 1986, I served on the Capitol Area Planning and Architectural Board (CAAPB) during Gov. Rudy Perpich's administration. For four years I enjoyed entering the Rotunda on a regular basis, admiring the governors' portraits, the green carpeted steps leading to the House of Representatives, the stately Governor's Office, and the amazing amount of marble all around.

Once I climbed up with others on the board to check on the golden horses of the *Progress of the State* quadriga, which needed repair. We often sat for hours with architectural advisor John

The Louis Hill House at 260 Summit Avenue,
dubbed Dove Hill by the Nicholsons

At the south end of Rice Park is the city's classically designed central library, renamed in honor of former mayor George Latimer.

Rauma, debating how we could keep the Capitol Mall intact, where to construct the next building, and which architecture firm would get the job.

Another of Saint Paul's main attractions is Summit Avenue, still the home of many of its leading citizens and now recognized as the last of America's Victorian boulevards. Walking along the historic street toward downtown, I admire the Burbank–Livingston–Griggs house (by Otis Wheelock, 1872), Fitzgerald's old haunts such as the University Club (by Allen H. Stem, 1913) , the Lightner house (by Cass Gilbert, 1894), Garrison Keillor's colonial revival house (the Lindsay–Weyerhaeuser house, 1919), and then pass by the restored Louis Hill residence (1903). F. Scott Fitzgerald and Sinclair Lewis lived at one time on Summit Avenue, too. Many of the oldest homes endure, their richly carved staircases intact. The avenue is a walk though the pages of history.

Some of the traditional rivalry between Saint Paul and Minneapolis remains, but residents present and past of the smaller, capital city claim certain bragging rights. My list includes Rice Park, the revitalized riverfronts, the Ordway Center for the Performing Arts, the old Women's City Club (an art deco gem by Marcus Jemne, 1931), and another masterwork of art deco—the Saint Paul City Hall and Ramsey County Courthouse (by Thomas Ellerbe & Company (later Ellerbe Becket) of Saint Paul and Holabird & Root of Chicago, 1932). Unforgettable is its Memorial Hall, housing the gigantic onyx statue *Vision of Peace,* a standout even in a room of black Belgian marble pillars.

That's only my short list; there's much more to see. But the structure that started it all for me was the old Pioneer Press Building, at Fourth Street and Minnesota, across the street from which my father, Whitey Jones, worked as a mailer/printer. It was there, at the age of 12, that I first met a couple of friendly reporters, heard the Linotype machines clacking away, and watched the presses roll. I decided to become a journalist. It's been a great adventure all the way.

The capital city, with its historic skyline, is very much the river city that attracted many early immigrants who then built a prosperous community on its riverbanks.

# Afterword: A Classy Bunch

I cannot complete this architectural retrospective without mentioning other Minnesota architects who are already making waves in the profession. I have known many of them in various ways and written about some of them. I commend all of them for their creation of lively and bolder-than-ever works of architecture in Minnesota and elsewhere. Watch for their innovative works yet to come:

- Joan Soranno is a singular designer, influenced by her work with Frank Gehry on the Weisman Art Museum in Minneapolis. She works with her husband, John Cook, creating and interchanging models, until the two agree on a proposed design. Joan's national award-winning Lakewood Cemetery Garden Mausoleum is an example of her finest minimalist work.
- James Dayton is a modernist at heart after working in his early professional years for Gehry. Dayton also loves resurrecting historic buildings to serve as restaurants and in other new ways.
- Tim Carl's redesign of Northrop Auditorium is a current triumph, as is his Ordway Concert Hall. Both demonstrate the soul of a great designer.
- Dale Mulfinger is a longtime leader of residential design and

the ultimate designer of cabins, cottages, swank lake homes, and others.

- Charles Stinson's signature designs feature sophisticated contemporary homes, many in a horizontal mode.
- Julie Snow's homes and other striking works demonstrate the power of simplicity in matching glass, cedar, and industrial materials to particular sites.
- Rosemary McMonigal mixes the traditional with modernism in home designs reflecting her clients' wishes.
- Lars Peterssen does excellent remodels of historic homes while showing a modernist streak in designing others.
- Tom Meyer's personal knowledge of the Minneapolis milling district and his intuitive design sense have given us the Mill City Museum, built within the shell of the Washburn "A" flourmill, once the largest in the world.
- Phillip Koski is a young preservationist who strives to save historic architecture through his remodels, additions, and insightful writing.
- Vincent James and Jennifer Yoos are recognized for the beauty of their minimalist style in homes (for example, the Judy Dayton house), structures near water, the Saint John's University guesthouse, and more.

A classy bunch, indeed! Watch for the names of these accomplished architects in the news as they continue to create new trends in preservation and architecture.

## ACKNOWLEDGMENTS

My special thanks go to Karen Melvin, for her indefatigable research for suitable black-and-white photos and her outstanding color photography, both original and acquired. I am also grateful for support throughout the process from friends such as: Jack Dietrich, daughter Susan Hammel, Gail See, Peggy Watson, Ken Wilcox, and Renata Winsor.

## PHOTO CREDITS

All illustrations are printed by permission.

Christian Öser – Cover photo
Pekka Agarth 86, 121
Americanspirit 202–203
Andrey Bayda 153
Trevor Benbrook 171
Gaston Bergeret 114
Michael Buckner 110
Mark Bulter 198–99
John Candelario, 156, Courtesy Palace of the Governors Photo Archives (NMHM-DCA)165657
Kobby Dagan 158
Songquan Deng 42-43
Fazlet Photo 127
Lakov Filimonov 128–29
Ann Fisher 191
Fotoember 116
Gunther Fraulob 125
Bette Hammel 29
Richard Hammel 31
Peter Hurley 133
Sophie James 122
Barbara Karant 125
Kasto 124
Brenda Kean 168
Lissandra Melo 178–79
Karen Melvin 10–11, 15, 18–19, 51, 60, 61, 64, 68, 69, 72, 76, 77, 80, 82, 90–91, 96-97, 103, 104, 116, 117, 118, 119, 120, 121, 122, 123, 130–31, 208–209, 210–211, 212, 214–15
Memitina 150
Victor Orlewicz 111
Alexandr Pakhnyushchyy 124
Lipskiy Pavel 132
PB Photos 146–47
Plus 99 142–43
Guven Polat 194–95
Philip Prowse 52–53, 55, 114, 116, 117, 123
Rognar 127
Tom Rossiter 174–75, 182–183
Science Museum of Minnesota 99
Mark Skalney 162–63
Walter Smith 101
Jose Ignacio Soto 115
Anthony Totah 113
Les Turneau 5, 113
David Pereiras Villagrá 152
Mike Waters 111

Illustration: Tim Carl, FAIA 22